P L A
T O B

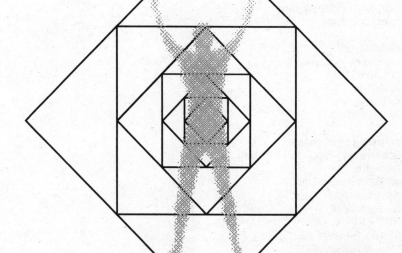

95/96

Includes ten venues in Ireland, France, Spain and Greece!

The Guide to Residential
Facilities with a Difference

Edited by Jonathan How

Places to Be 95/96
The Guide to Residential Facilities
with a Difference

ISBN
0 9524396 0 3

© Coherent Visions 1994

Editor and Designer
Jonathan How

Publisher
Coherent Visions
PO Box 1808
Winslow
Buckingham
MK18 3RN

Printer (contents)
Greenwood Recycled Printing
Lakeside
off Warehouse Hill
Marsden
Huddersfield
HD7 6AE
01484 844841

Printer (cover)
Buckingham Colour Press
Riverside Works
Bridge Street
Buckingham
MK18 1EN
01280 824000

Distributor
(trade and mail order)
Edge of Time Ltd
PO Box 1808
Winslow
Buckingham
MK18 3RN

Contents

Introduction

A phenomenon has been quietly bubbling under the surface for the last two decades - it may or may not be a millennial trend! Every weekend (and quite often during the week as well) many people are, of their own volition, attending residential courses in the fields of personal growth, healing and alternative lifestyles. Subjects range from growing vegetables to growing yourself; from learning about a craft to learning about a spiritual path.

This book is, primarily, a guide to a whole new type of residential venue which has sprung up to cater for this market. Typically it offers facilities which are a lot less boring than the average hotel or conference centre. More importantly these kinds of places offer an ambience which is conducive to learning, exploration and development.Standards of physical accommodation may vary but quality of food is usually a top priority (you are what you eat after all!) with catering for special diets a major concern.

If these venues have one thing in common it is that they provide a place away from the hubbub of the everyday world where course participants can reflect and experiment with new ways of being and doing. This quality makes them increasingly attractive to mainstream organisations which now recognise the value of taking staff out of the working environment in order to gain perspective and cope better with change.

Information about these places is around and about, it is not particularly hidden. But it's very disparate. *Places to BE* is an attempt to bring that information together in one handy guide. Its aim is to become the essential reference in the field of life transforming workshops, holidays and events. A selection of more traditional religious retreat houses have been included; as have several alternative style B&Bs. Workshop facilities are at the core of this guide but these other kinds of venues may well be included in greater numbers in future editions.

This is very much a pilot. It feels as if it is important to present the broad idea and get feedback on it in order to enhance its future development. So please let me know what you think about it and what it is that *you* are looking for from a guide like this. It's particularly important for me to hear the views of both the people who are (generally) participants in workshops and those that run and/or organise them.

This is not in any way an"Egon Ronay style" guide. Each venue has written its own entry. I cannot take responsibility for the accuracy of entries as I am not in a position to verify anything more than the basic information sent to me. (I should also point out that I cannot be held

Introduction

responsible for anything that may occur to individuals visiting the venues in this directory. If you have a negative experience of a particular venue then by all means tell me but the maximum penalty I could enforce would be to exclude them from a future edition.)

On a more positive note - please encourage venues that are not included to get in touch with me. I am aware of several notable omissions - places that just did not respond to my endless reminders. If you find a place through this book then please also tell that venue that you read about it in *Places to BE*. It will help me the next time when they're deciding whether to fill their entry form in straight away or lose it behind the filing cabinet!

I hope that all *your* experiences are truly transformational and look forward to receiving your postcards ... and the one at the back of the book!

Jonathan How, Michaelmas 1994

Acknowledgements
Thanks to all those venues that sent in entries so enthusiastically! I'd also like to thank Ulrike and Belinda at Neal's Yard Agency for their encouraging response; my fellow co-operators at the edge of time; and last but by no means least: Michelle, Chris, Sue, Shirley and Simon for their exhaustive proof-reading.

Ways in

If you are new to this whole area and do not know where to begin then a good starting point are the magazines listed below. Many of them also carry advertisements for workshops and courses.

This first group deal with green issues and tend to operate more on the material plane:

Alternative Green
20 Upper Barr, Cowley Centre, OXFORD, OX4 3UX

Clean Slate
care of C A T, Llwyngwern Quarry, MACHYNLLETH, Powys, SY20 9AZ

Earth Matters
26 to 28 Underwood Street, LONDON, N1 7JQ
0171 490 1555

Green Drum
18 Cofton Lake Road, BIRMINGHAM, B45 8PL

Green Line
Catalyst Collective Ltd, 82 Andover Street, SHEFFIELD, S3 9EH

Green Magazine
PO Box 381, Millharbour, LONDON, E14 9TW
0171 987 5090

H D R A Newsletter
Nat Centre for Organic Gardening, Ryton-on-Dunsmore, COVENTRY, CV8 3LG
01203 303517

Living Green
23 Springfield Road, GUILDFORD, GU1 4DW
01483 67191

Peace News
5 Caledonian Road, LONDON,
N1 9DX
0171 278 3344
Permaculture Magazine
Hyden House, Little Hyden Lane,
CLANFIELD, Hampshire, PO8 0RU
01705 596500
W W O O F News
87 Oak Road, Horfield, BRISTOL,
BS7 8RZ
0117 942 1849

*This second group of magazines
deal more with spirituality,
healing and the human potential
movement ... but that does not
mean that they are not interested
in green issues!*
Caduceus
38 Russell Terrace, ROYAL
LEAMINGTON SPA, Warwickshire,
CV31 1HE
01926 451897
Cahoots
PO Box 12, Levenshulme PDO,
MANCHESTER, M19 2EW
Community
Woodbrooke Coll,1046 Bristol
Road, Selly Oak, BIRMINGHAM,
B29 6LJ
0121 472 8079
Connections
Laurel Cottage, Watery Lane,
DONHEAD St MARY, Dorset,
SP7 9DF
01747 828913
The Friend
Drayton House, 30 Gordon Street,
LONDON, WC1H 0BQ
0171 387 7549
Human Potential
5 Layton Road, LONDON, N1 0PX
0171 354 5792

I to I: The Alternative Magazine
92 Prince of Wales Road,
LONDON, NW5 3NE
0171 267 7094
Insight
PO Box 490, HOVE, Sussex, BN3 3BU
01273 726970
Kindred Spirit
Foxhole, Dartington, TOTNES,
Devon, TQ9 6EB
01803 866686
Mind Body Soul
Enigma Associates Ltd,
405 Croydon Road, BECKENHAM,
Kent, BR3 3PR
0181 663 3007
New Humanity
51a York Mansions, Prince of
Wales Drive, LONDON, SW11 4BP
0171 622 4013
One Earth
The Findhorn Press, The Park,
FORRES , Morayshire, IV36 0TZ
01309 690010
Planetary Connections
PO Box 44, EVESHAM,
Worcestershire, WR12 7YW
01386 858694
Rainbow Ark Magazine
PO Box 486, LONDON, SW1P 1AZ
0171 266 0175
Resurgence
Ford House, BIDEFORD, Devon,
EX39 6EE
01237 441293
Sacred Hoop
28 Cowl Street, EVESHAM,
Worcestershire, WR11 4PL
01824 702271

And then of course there is:
Time Out
Tower House, Southampton St,
LONDON, WC2E 7HD
0171 836 4411

14 Neal's Yard
Covent Garden
London WC2H 9DP
Tel: 0171 379 0141   Fax: 0171 379 0135

Are you running your own workshops?
Do you need help with putting the word out?

*Neal's Yard Agency for Personal Development
lets the public and the media know what courses and
trainings are available. They can help you with promotional
activities and also offer you the chance to use their Central
London Meeting Rooms as a venue.*

For workshop leaders there are opportunities to:

❥ *display posters and leaflets in the Covent Garden Shop*

❥ *reach 5000 people on their constantly updated mailing
list with a listing, flyer or a feature*

❥ *offer potential clients a sample of your work in a Neal's
Yard "Taster" workshop*

... and much more ...

They can promote your work wherever
you practice, including holidays abroad.

If you would like to know more
contact Ulrike Speyer on
0171 379 0141

Neal's Yard Agency for Personal Development

14 Neal's Yard
Covent Garden
London WC2H 9DP
Tel: 0171 379 0141 Fax: 0171 379 0135

The Travel Agent
for Inner Journeys

a one stop shop

for hundreds of
- *courses*
- *workshops*
- *holidays*

*also offering free advice on
personal development*

- **Meditation**
- **Tai Ji**
- **Yoga**
- **Drum**
- **Dance**
- **Holidays**

How to use the Directory

The main body of the Directory is contained in the Regional Listings which begin on page 21. A typical entry looks like this:

the name of the venue - this will usually be the name of the building although in some cases organisational names have been given

they offer retreats of some kind but you need to check up with them whether they are for individuals or groups, whether they are guided or DIY

they offer residential facilities for hire to external group organisers and leaders

they offer their own workshops and/or courses, get them to send you a course programme

The Manor House

- ☑ **Retreats**
- ☑ **Venue**
- ☑ **Workshops**
- ☑ **Bed & Breakfast**

6 bedspaces in 3 rooms

North Street
Beaminster
Dorset
DT8 3DZ
Telephone: 01308 862311
Facsimile: 01308 862311

This elegant house provides a special place for guests to relax in the peace and quiet of the Dorset countryside.

they offer bed and breakfast to the general public, however in many cases this is unlikely to be available on demand so always make a firm booking before travelling

this is the number of bedrooms over which the bedspaces are spread - this will give you a rough idea of how many people have to share a room, contact the venue for more detailed information

this is the number of bedspaces available - some places may be able to handle more people ... but in less salubrious conditions!

☑ **Retreats**

People from all religions have been going on retreats for hundreds, if not thousands, of years. As the pace of life in the industrialised world speeds up this ancient form of getting away from it all has suddenly started to rise in popularity again. What's more, often amongst people who are not necessarily attached to a particular religion.

Many Christian establishments cater for this demand, often on quite a large scale. Some of those places are listed but by no means all. Some felt that a publication such as this was not appropriate for them.

There are however a growing number of smaller venues offering retreats - and, hopefully, this is just the publication for them. Within the context of this first edition a broad brush approach has been used and when a venue says that it offers retreats you will need to check exactly what they mean.

You need to check whether the retreats are for individuals or groups; whether they are based on any particular spiritual system; how much guidance is available and/or how much you will be left to your own devices.

☑ **Venue**

If you run courses or workshops yourself then it's these tickboxes that you'll be looking out for.

You may already have a region in mind in which case you're probably best to turn straight to the Regional Listings and start browsing. You'll soon become aware that some regions are better served than others!

On the other hand you may be starting from the numbers end. Decide your approximate range then turn to the Index by Size which begins on page 14. Venues are listed in ascending order according to the number of bedspaces. The information in *Places to BE* is meant to be a starting point, so there is no detail on numbers of twin/ triplet/ quadruplet rooms etc. However, you will be able to get a rough idea from the ratio of bedspaces to rooms. Contact the venue for more details.

The Index by Size shows a ◆ in the *Venue?* column if that particular place offers facilities for hire. The region and page number of the detailed entry are shown at the end of the line.

☑ Workshops

If you are a budding workshop participant then you're going to be thumbing through the Regional Listings looking for all the places with this tickbox.

Venues that run workshops and/or courses will often describe the subject areas in which they specialise in their written description. You will need to write or phone to obtain a more definite course programme from them.

There is no categorisation according to subject areas in this edition of *Places to BE* - if this is something that you would find particularly useful then please mention it when you send in your reply-paid card (to be found at the back of the book).

Perhaps you've already booked for a workshop and want to find out a bit more about the place where it's going to be held. If this is the case you can look it up in the Index by Name section which begins on page 108.

☑ Bed & Breakfast

The B&Bs listed in *Places to BE* are all distinctive in some way, even if that way is simply that they offer vegetarian food. The list does not, however, claim to be comprehensive in any way (for instance there are a number of very good vegetarian B&B guides already, containing hundreds of addresses, and it would be pointless to replicate them).

Many of those in *Places to BE* are representative of a new breed of B&B which offer something more than just food and accommodation. Perhaps it is some kind of educational service, perhaps a healing therapy. This is a growing area and future editions of this book will hopefully chart the increasing numbers of venues operating in this field.

Index by Size

Venue	Number of bedspaces	Number of rooms	Retreats?	Venue for hire?	Workshops?	Bed & Breakfast?	Region	Page number
Great Burrow	2	1	◆				South West England	80
Dyemill Studio	3	1					Scotland	24
Bowthorpe Comm Trust	3	2	◆			◆	East Anglia	51
Castle Cottage	3	2	◆		◆	◆	East Anglia	52
Glyn y Mel	4	2	◆			◆	Wales	67
Peace Haven	4	3	◆				South East England	90
Brakes Coppice Farm	5	3	◆			◆	South East England	94
Divya-Krupa	5	3				◆	South East England	93
Little Ash Eco-Farm	5	3	◆	◆	◆	◆	South West England	79
Hope House	6	3	◆		◆	◆	South West England	78
The Manor House	6	3	◆	◆	◆	◆	South West England	76
Rumwood	6	3	◆	◆	◆	◆	East Anglia	49
Yeo Cottage	6	3	◆			◆	South West England	83
The Centre of Light	6	4	◆		◆		Scotland	26
Community of St Peters	6	4	◆	◆			Greater London	98

Places to BE

Name						Region	Page
Waterfall Cottage	6	4		◆	◆	South West England	77
Poor Clares	6	6	◆		◆	Wales	65
The Eden Centre	7	3	◆	◆		South West England	81
Tregeraint House	7	3	◆		◆	South West England	85
The Barn	7	7	◆	◆		South West England	83
Le Blé en Herbe	8	3	◆	◆	◆	Outside the UK	103
Le Plessis	8	3	◆		◆	Outside the UK	103
Tabor Trust	8	4	◆	◆		Scotland	28
Wolfscastle Pottery	8	5	◆	◆	◆	Wales	66
Amadeus Hotel	9	5			◆	Yorkshire & Humberside	45
Jenny's Bothy	10	2	◆	◆		Scotland	26
Rivendell Community	10	3	◆			North West England	39
Boswednack Manor	10	5	◆	◆	◆	South West England	85
Eller Close	10	5	◆	◆	◆	Northern England	33
The Sanctuary	10	5	◆	◆	◆	Outside the UK	106
Shambhala	10	5	◆	◆	◆	South West England	77
West Usk Lighthouse	10	6	◆	◆	◆	Wales	68
Hinton House	10	8	◆		◆	South West England	75
A Badger's Rest	12	4	◆	◆	◆	Northern England	33
Earthworm	12	4	◆	◆		West Midlands	61
Nightingale Light Cntre	12	5	◆	◆	◆	South West England	78

Venue	Number of bedspaces	Number of rooms	Retreats?	Venue for hire?	Workshops?	Bed & Breakfast?	Region	Page number
Tidicombe House	12	6	◆	◆	◆	◆	South West England	80
The Rowan Tree Centre	13	7	◆		◆		Wales	65
Talamh	14	3	◆	◆	◆		Scotland	24
Upper Vanley	14	6	◆	◆	◆	◆	Wales	66
Woodcote Hotel	14	6				◆	South West England	85
Christian Holiday Cntre	14	7	◆	◆	◆	◆	Wales	65
The Old Mill	14	9	◆	◆	◆		South West England	83
The Old Stable House	14	9	◆	◆	◆		East Anglia	50
Samadhan	14		◆	◆	◆		Scotland	25
White Edge Lodge	15	3	◆	◆	◆		East Midlands	55
Domaine de Magot	15	6	◆	◆		◆	Outside the UK	105
Holy Rood House	15	10	◆	◆	◆	◆	Yorkshire & Humberside	43
East Down Centre	16	4		◆			South West England	82
Domaine de Montfleuri	16	5			◆	◆	Outside the UK	105
Red Water Centre	16	5	◆	◆	◆		North West England	40

Name					Region	
Redfield Centre	16	5	◆		South East England	90
Quiraing Lodge	16	7	◆	◆	Scotland	25
Parkfield Guest House	16	8	◆	◆	Northern England	35
Turvey Abbey	16	13	◆		South East England	90
Bainesbury House	17	4	◆		South West England	76
Woodwick House	17	9	◆	◆	Scotland	26
St Michael's Convent	17	15	◆		Greater London	99
Little Grove	18	4	◆		South East England	91
Columbanus Community	18	6	◆		Northern Ireland	30
Fawcett Mill Fields	18	8	◆		Northern England	34
Lios Dána	18	8	◆	◆	Outside the UK	102
Nunnery House Hotel	18	9		◆	Northern England	35
Pitt White	18	9	◆	◆	South West England	75
Kilnwick Percy Hall	19	8	◆	◆	Yorkshire & Humberside	43
Braziers Adult College	19	13	◆		South East England	92
Anybody's Barn	20	5	◆		West Midlands	59
Beech Hill Community	20	6	◆	◆	South West England	78
Manoir les Thomas	20	8	◆	◆	Outside the UK	104
Stacklands	20	20	◆		South East England	95
Water Hall	21	8	◆		East Anglia	51
Cortijo Romero	22	11	◆		Outside the UK	106

Venue	Number of bedspaces	Number of rooms	Retreats?	Venue for hire?	Workshops?	Bed & Breakfast?	Region	Page number
Le Relais	22	11				◆	Outside the UK	102
Mountain Hall Centre	23	13		◆	◆		Yorkshire & Humberside	45
Taraloka	24	5	◆		◆		West Midlands	61
St Katharine	24	20	◆	◆	◆		Greater London	98
Wild Pear Centre	25	5	◆	◆	◆		South West England	81
C A E R	25	10	◆	◆	◆	◆	South West England	84
Newbold House	28	10	◆	◆	◆		Scotland	27
Runnings Park	28	22	◆	◆	◆	◆	West Midlands	60
St Denys Retreat Centre	28	22	◆	◆	◆		South West England	73
Houghton Chapel	30	6	◆	◆			East Anglia	49
The Beacon Centre	30	11	◆	◆	◆	◆	South West England	82
Pluscarden Abbey	30	26	◆				Scotland	27
Four Winds Centre	32	9	◆	◆	◆		South East England	93
The Grail	32	17	◆	◆	◆		Greater London	100
Pen Rhiw	33	20	◆	◆			Wales	67

Name								Region	
Offa House	33	26			♦	♦	♦	West Midlands	59
Monkton Wyld Court	34	11		♦	♦	♦	♦	South West England	75
Ashton Lodge	37	18		♦	♦	♦		South West England	74
Springhead Trust	39	8		♦	♦	♦		South West England	76
The Cenacle	39	30		♦	♦	♦		South East England	93
Unstone Grange	40	10		♦	♦	♦		East Midlands	59
Grimstone Manor	40	13		♦	♦	♦		South West England	84
Lower Shaw Farm	40	15		♦	♦	♦		South West England	73
Ickwell Bury	40	17		♦	♦	♦		South East England	90
Ruth White Yoga Centre	40	30		♦	♦	♦	♦	Greater London	99
Campion House	40	40		♦	♦	♦		Greater London	100
Barhaugh Hall	43	25		♦	♦	♦	♦	Northern England	36
Kirkby Fleetham Hall	46	22		♦	♦	♦	♦	Yorkshire & Humberside	44
Bore Place	48	27		♦	♦	♦	♦	South East England	94
Mickleton House	50	25		♦	♦	♦		South West England	72
Hawkwood College	52	32		♦	♦	♦	♦	South West England	72
Dhamma Dipa	60	24	♦	♦	♦	♦		West Midlands	60
Birchcliffe Centre	62	16			♦	♦		Yorkshire & Humberside	45
Wydale Hall	67	34		♦	♦	♦	♦	Yorkshire & Humberside	44
Laurieston Hall	70	11		♦	♦	♦		Scotland	24
Spirit Horse Camps	80	13		♦	♦	♦		Wales	65

Index by Size

Venue	Number of bedspaces	Number of rooms	Retreats?	Venue for hire?	Workshops?	Bed & Breakfast?	Region	Page number
High Lea	80	14		◆	◆		South West England	74
Carberry	90	40		◆	◆		Scotland	28
Aylesford Priory	100	62	◆	◆	◆	◆	South East England	95
Harborne Hall	100	74		◆			West Midlands	59
Gaunts House	120	45	◆	◆	◆	◆	South West England	74
Comm of All Hallows	120		◆	◆	◆		East Anglia	51
Emerson College	140	140	◆	◆	◆		South East England	94
Findhorn Foundation	150				◆		Scotland	27
Skyros Centre - Atsitsa	160	80	◆		◆		Outside the UK	106
Hill End	179	26		◆	◆		South East England	92
Dartington Hall	280	260		◆		◆	South West England	83
Vegiventures							Outside the UK	107

Scotland

Scotland

The drawing on the previous page shows the stone circle at Callanish on the Isle of Lewis

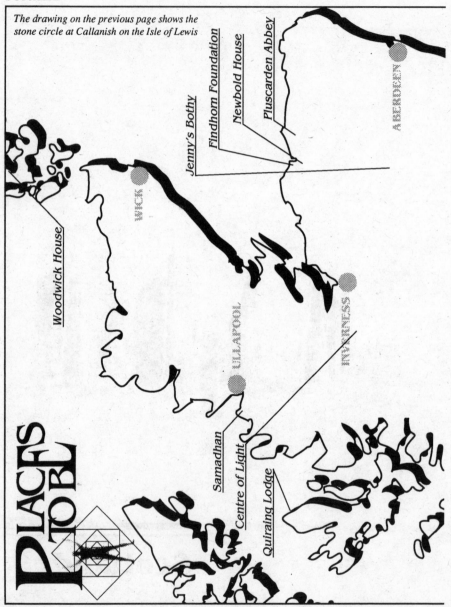

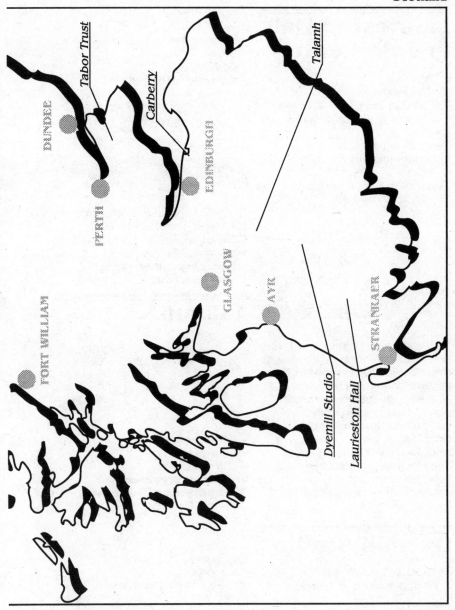

DUNDEE

Tabor Trust

Carberry

Talamh

PERTH

EDINBURGH

FORT WILLIAM

GLASGOW

AYR

STRANRAER

Dyemill Studio

Laurieston Hall

Laurieston Hall People Centre

☑ **Venue**
☑ **Workshops**
70 bedspaces in 11 rooms
Laurieston Hall People Centre
Laurieston
Castle Douglas
Kirkcudbrightshire
DG7 2NB
Telephone: 01644 450633
Facsimile: 01644 450633

We are a rural community with over 100 acres of woodland; riverside; lochside; moorland and pasture; swimming and sauna. Members co-operate to run residential events; family holidays; courses in theatre, circus skills, dance, music, singing, t'ai chi, healing and therapy; gay and lesbian events. Food is mostly home grown organic. For details write for annual newsletter.

Dyemill Studio

☑ **Bed & Breakfast**
3 bedspaces in 1 room
Dyemill Studio
Dyemill
Sidmount Avenue
Moffat
DG10 9BS
Telephone: 01683 20681

Delightful spacious stone cottage for couple/small family. Self catering/vegetarian B&B. Evening meal available. Beautiful surroundings. No smoking. Colour television.

Talamh

☑ **Retreats**
☑ **Venue**
☑ **Workshops**
☑ **Bed & Breakfast**
14 bedspaces in 3 rooms
Contact: Janie Kyle
Talamh
Birkhill House
Coalburn
Lanarkshire
ML11 0NJ
Telephone: 01555 820555

Talamh is set in the Lanarkshire countryside in Scotland. We have a 16th Century house set in 50 acres of land which is managed as a species habitat coupled with fun and education. Our facilities include bunk room accommodation, camping and workshop space for courses. We cook vegetarian food with fresh organic vegetables from our own garden. We also cater for vegan diets. Talamh is always open to new ideas and ventures. Talamh awaits.

We are an open retreat centre and vegetarian B&B set in the spectacular scenery of north east Skye. We have seven twin-bedded rooms for individual retreats or as a group venue. We specialise in a relaxed family atmosphere, and offer our own programme of retreats as well as taking groups with their own programme.

Samadhan

Quiraing Lodge

☑ **Retreats**
☑ **Venue**
☑ **Workshops**
☑ **Bed & Breakfast**
16 bedspaces in 7 rooms
Contact: Kate Money
Quiraing Lodge
Staffin
Isle of Skye
IV51 9JS
Telephone: 01470 562330

☑ **Retreats**
☑ **Venue**
☑ **Workshops**
14 bedspaces
Contact: Sundara Forsyth
Samadhan
Scoraig Peninsula
Garve
Dundonnell
Wester Ross
IV23 2RE
Telephone: 01854 633260

Beautiful, intimate venue in remote highland setting. Open year round. Accommodates 14 maximum ... write for leaflet. Access boat or footpath.

Woodwick House

☑ **Retreats**
☑ **Venue**
☑ **Workshops**
☑ **Bed & Breakfast**
17 bedspaces in 9 rooms
Contact: Ann Herdman
Woodwick House
Evie
Orkney
KW17 2PQ
Telephone: 01856 751330
Set in beautiful archipeligeo, own bay, seal watching, birds and woodland. Peace, good food, ancient sites. In Good Hotel Guide 1994.

The Centre of Light

☑ **Retreats**
☑ **Workshops**
6 bedspaces in 4 rooms

Contact: Linda Christie
The Centre of Light
Tighna Bruaich
Struy
by Beauly
Inverness-shire
IV4 7JU
Telephone: 01463 761 254
The Centre of Light is based in the Scottish Highlands and offers you somewhere to have a break away from the routine and stress of life. Here you can enjoy the peace of natural surroundings. The gentle landscape of the glen, surrounded by the mountain wilderness, provides many different environments to experience and find a key to your own inner self. We run workshops and retreats throughout the year, drawing from a wide range of experience in therapy, mediation and healing to create a unique programme for every visitor. Food is vegetarian, organic where possible, and accommodation is in a very comfortable B&B close to the Centre.

Jenny's Bothy

☑ **Retreats**
☑ **Venue**
☑ **Workshops**
10 bedspaces in 2 rooms
Jenny's Bothy
Dellachuper
Corgarff
Strathdon
Aberdeenshire
AB36 8YP
Telephone: 019756 51446

Beautiful unusual self-catering accommodation "where the wild things know no fear"! Paradise for children, occasional venue for workshops, courses. The accommodation comprises all basic amenities: electric cooker, fridge, wood-burning stove in a converted barn, and sleeps up to ten in two rooms. Available to be booked by individuals or groups. Visit local castles; gardens; stone circles; the Strathfest - a music and arts festival; or cross-country and downhill ski in winter.

Findhorn Foundation

☑ **Workshops**
150 bedspaces
Findhorn Foundation
Cluny Hill College
Forres
Morayshire
IV36 0RD
Telephone: 01309 673655
Facsimile: 01309 673113

An international spiritual community first known for work with plants, since become a centre for holistic education. Extensive workshop programme.

Newbold House

☑ **Retreats**
☑ **Workshops**
28 bedspaces in 10 rooms
Newbold House
St Leonards Road
Forres, Morayshire
IV36 0RE
Telephone: 01309 672659
NewBold House is a working spiritual community which welcomes guests to join in community life and educational workshops. It offers an integrated experience of living and relating in a different way. The atmosphere created in this beautiful old mansion house and its seven acres of woodland and gardens provides a caring and nurturing environment for individual self-exploration and growth.

Pluscarden Abbey

☑ **Retreats**
30 bedspaces in 26 rooms
Contact: Guestmaster/Warden
Pluscarden Abbey
Elgin, Morayshire
IV30 3UA
Telephone: 01343 89257
Facsimile: 01343 89258

Scotland

Pluscarden Abbey is a Benedictine monastery. The monks are contemplatives of the orthodox catholic tradition. Men's and women's retreat facilities.

Tabor Trust Retreat Centre

☑ **Retreats**
☑ **Venue**
☑ **Workshops**
8 bedspaces in 4 rooms
Contact: Lynda Wright
Tabor Trust Retreat Centre
Key House
High Street
Falkland
Fife
KY7 7BU
Telephone: 01337 857705

An ecumenical retreat house with four twin rooms which can be booked singly, situated beside Falkland Palace. Lovely walks, charming village, suitable for quiet breaks, individual or small group retreats, day workshops for up to twelve. Monthly weekend programmed events.

Carberry

☑ **Venue**
☑ **Workshops**
90 bedspaces in 40 rooms
Carberry
Musselburgh
Midlothian
EH21 8PY
Telephone: 0131 665 3135
Facsimile: 0131 653 2930

Carberry is a Scottish castle in lovely parkland, moving from Church of Scotland to independent status. A homely place used by people from all over the world. Inclusive Christian ethos.

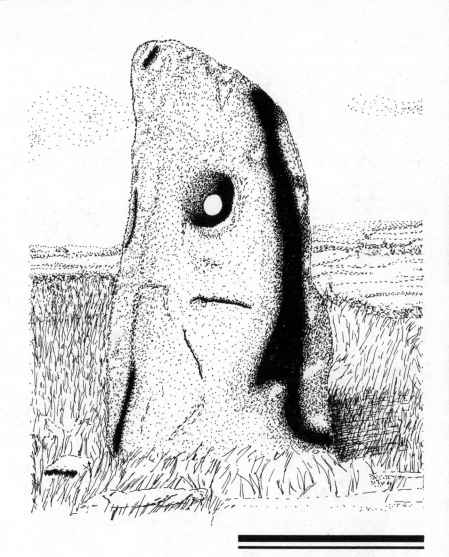

Northern
Ireland

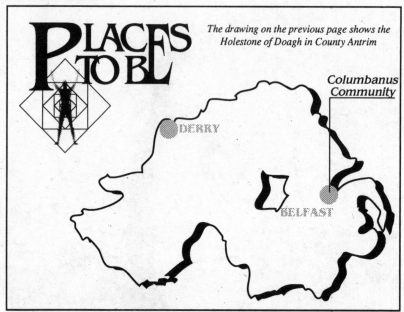

PLACES TO BE

The drawing on the previous page shows the Holestone of Doagh in County Antrim

Columbanus
Community

DERRY

BELFAST

Columbanus Community of Reconciliation

☑ **Retreats**
☑ **Venue**
☑ **Workshops**
18 bedspaces in 6 rooms
Contact: Roisin Hannaway
Columbanus Community of Reconciliation
683 Antrim Road
Belfast
BT15 4EG
Telephone: 01232 778009
An ecumenical residential community of men and women, Catholics and Protestants. Full or self-catering accommodation for individuals or married couples who wish to learn more about the work of reconciliation in Northern Ireland. Opportunity for quiet, for use of library and garden, for participation in community prayer. Also self-catering Youth Annexe for twelve. Community membership open to Christians who could give a year or more to the work of reconciliation in Belfast.

Northern
England

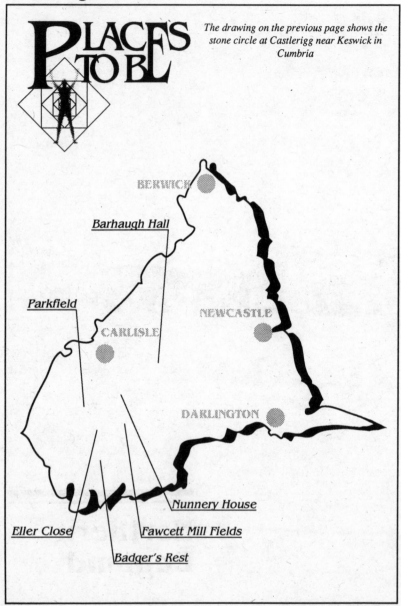

PLACE'S TO BE

The drawing on the previous page shows the stone circle at Castlerigg near Keswick in Cumbria

BERWICK

Barhaugh Hall

Parkfield

NEWCASTLE

CARLISLE

DARLINGTON

Nunnery House

Eller Close

Fawcett Mill Fields

Badger's Rest

Eller Close Vegetarian Guest House

☑ **Retreats**
☑ **Venue**
☑ **Bed & Breakfast**
10 bedspaces in 5 rooms
Eller Close
Grasmere
Cumbria
LA22 9RW
Telephone: 015394 35 786

Charming Victorian house in delightful secluded gardens with mountain stream. Wonderful views from every room. Delicious cooked breakfast. Non smoking.

A Badger's Rest

☑ **Retreats**
☑ **Venue**
☑ **Workshops**
☑ **Bed & Breakfast**
12 bedspaces in 4 rooms

Contact: Paula Badger
A Badger's Rest
Bankfield
Ings
near Windermere
Cumbria
LA8 9PY
Telephone: 01539 821135
Facsimile: 01539 821135

Hotel specialising in vegetarian gourmet food. Evening from £17.95 to £25.95. Also courses for husbands, children, hostesses who need inspiration. Organic farm foods and wines used predominately; vegetarian and vegan food. Open to non-residents. Chef/Proprietor is author of recipes to be printed by Salmon Publishers of Mrs Badger's Lakeland Crumbles fame. Compiling menus for accreditation with the Vegetarian Society and Soil Association. Guest can stay for as little as £17.50 per night standard. En-suite with half-tester bed and balcony, would suit honeymoon couple or family: £22.50 per person. Children under eight half price. Menus created to suit likes and dislikes of a European and Far Eastern style. Six courses including home proved unusual breads. For breakfast try our girdle almond cakes. Ours is a delightful place for food critics, lovers of good tasting food and wines, hospitality and personal attention. Champagne picnics and balloon trips catered for. Each guest takes away their own personalised menu for each evening - attractive enough to frame!

Fawcett Mill Fields

- ☑ **Retreats**
- ☑ **Venue**
- ☑ **Workshops**

18 bedspaces in 8 rooms

Contact: Sue Wallace
Fawcett Mill Fields
Gaisgill, Tebay
Penrith, Cumbria
CA10 3UB
Telephone: 015396 24408

Fawcett Mill Fields offers you an environment for calm reflection and reconnection with the rythms of nature. Set in an idyllic situation by a waterfall, there is a stunning group room plus two sitting rooms. The centre is warm, comfortable and feels like a home away from home. All diets catered for.

Nunnery House Hotel

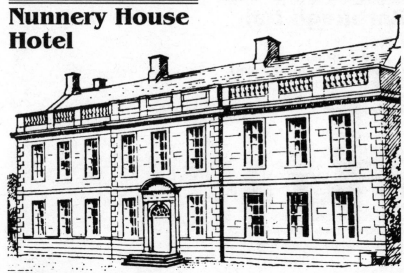

☑ **Venue**
☑ **Bed & Breakfast**
18 bedspaces in 9 rooms
Contact: Joan Armstrong
Nunnery House Hotel
Staffield
Kirkoswald
Penrith
Cumbria
CA10 1EU
Telephone: 01768 898537
We offer peace and quiet to individuals or groups in an ancient nunnery. Set in own grounds with waterfalls.

Parkfield Guest House

☑ **Venue**
☑ **Bed & Breakfast**
16 bedspaces in 8 rooms

Parkfield Guest House
The Heads
Keswick, Cumbria
CA12 5ES
Telephone: 01768 772328
In a superb location with mountain views half way between town and lake, Parkfield - a turn of the century lakeland residence - enjoys great light and tranquility. Family run as a guest-house, David and Valerie have established a growing reputation for vegetarian, vegan and macrobiotic specialities. With car park, eight double bedrooms (most with facilities) and large airy lounge, it provides an ideal base for short or long-term breaks, walking, outdoor activities and small workshops. Telephone for a brochure.

Barhaugh Hall

☑ **Venue**
☑ **Bed & Breakfast**
43 bedspaces in 25 rooms
Contact: Carol Brack
Barhaugh Hall
Kirkhaugh
Alston
Cumbria
CA9 3NJ
Telephone: 01434 381978
Facsimile: 01434 382004

Dedicated training facility with five conference and four syndicate rooms. Fabulous location in North Pennines Area of Outstanding Natural Beauty.

North West
England

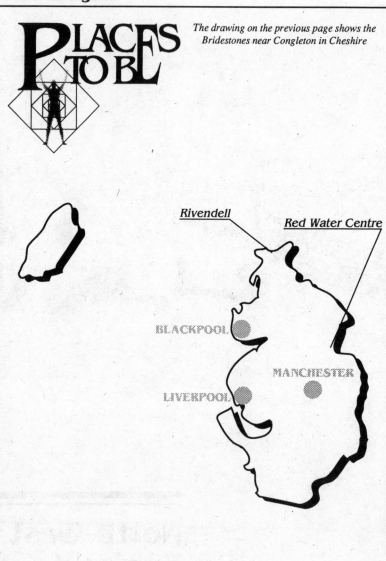

PLACES TO BE

*The drawing on the previous page shows the
Bridestones near Congleton in Cheshire*

Rivendell

Red Water Centre

BLACKPOOL

MANCHESTER

LIVERPOOL

Rivendell Community

☑ **Retreats**
10 bedspaces in 3 rooms
Contact: Noel or Jean Charlton
Rivendell Community
Rigmaden Farmhouse
Mansergh
Carnforth
Lancashire
LA6 2ET
Telephone: 015242 76265

We offer up to two weeks of space, healing and rest to those needing respite from stress, illness or loneliness. Rivendell is a Christian family household where we share a rural lifestyle and beautiful countryside with our guests. There is time to talk, listen, walk, ride, read or make music. Please phone daytime or early evening for details.

Red Water Centre

☑ **Venue**
☑ **Workshops**
16 bedspaces in 5 rooms
Red Water Centre
Back Rough Farm
Coalclough Road
Todmorden
Lancashire
OL14 8NU
Telephone: 01706 815328

The farmhouse centre is surrounded by woods, hills and tumbling waters. It offers accommodation with workshop facilities for hire. Our food is excellent but groups may wish to be self catering. Please write for a brochure.

Yorkshire
and
Humberside

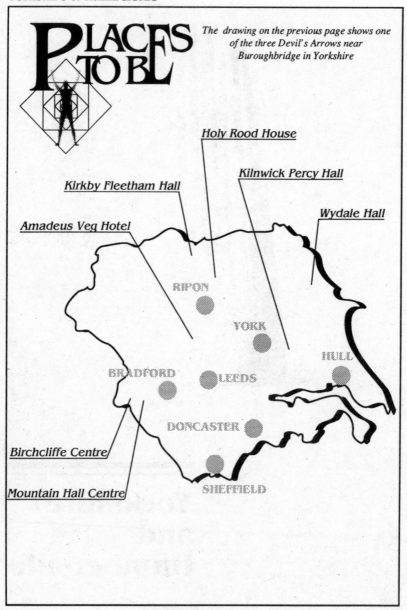

Places to Be

The drawing on the previous page shows one of the three Devil's Arrows near Buroughbridge in Yorkshire

Holy Rood House

Kilnwick Percy Hall

Kirkby Fleetham Hall

Wydale Hall

Amadeus Veg Hotel

RIPON

YORK

HULL

BRADFORD

LEEDS

DONCASTER

Birchcliffe Centre

Mountain Hall Centre

SHEFFIELD

Kilnwick Percy Hall

☑ **Retreats**
☑ **Workshops**
☑ **Bed & Breakfast**
19 bedspaces in 8 rooms
Madhyamaka Buddhist Centre
Kilnwick Percy Hall
Pocklington
York
YO4 2UF
Telephone: 01759 304832
Facsimile: 01759 305962

This elegant Georgian hall in the Wolds houses a residential community of fifty lay and ordained people studying, practising and teaching New Kaoampa Buddhism. Single, double and dormitory accommodation. Vegetarian meals. Working holidays possible. Everyone welcome.

Holy Rood House

☑ **Retreats**
☑ **Venue**
☑ **Workshops**
☑ **Bed & Breakfast**
15 bedspaces in 10 rooms
Contact: Rev Elizabeth or Rev Stanley Baxter

Holy Rood House
10 Sowerby Road
Thirsk
North Yorkshire
YO7 1HX
Telephone: 01845 522580
This lovely house, set in creative grounds, is the home of Healing and Peace, set up by The North of England Christian Healing Trust. Offering professional counselling and therapies and exploration of spirituality. We welcome all kinds of people of all ages on a donations basis with excellent home cooking (for all diets) or self-catering. We have a commitment to justice, peace and integrity of creation; an excellent library; two informal chapels; and animals share the house and gardens.

Wydale Hall

- ☑ **Retreats**
- ☑ **Venue**
- ☑ **Workshops**
- ☑ **Bed & Breakfast**

67 bedspaces in 34 rooms

Wydale Hall
Wydale Lane
Brompton by Sawdon
Scarborough
North Yorkshire
YO13 9DG
Telephone: 01723 859270
Facsimile: 01723 859702

Wydale, the York Diocesan Centre, is situated within 14 acres of grounds with woodlands. Ideal for retreats, quiet days, conferences, holidays. Accommodation for 67 guests - groups or individuals.

Kirkby Fleetham Hall

- ☑ **Retreats**
- ☑ **Venue**
- ☑ **Workshops**
- ☑ **Bed & Breakfast**

46 bedspaces in 22 rooms

Kirkby Fleetham Hall
Kirkby Fleetham
North Allerton
North Yorkshire
DL7 0SU
Telephone: 01609 748711
Facsimile: 01609 748747

Kirkby Fleetham Hall is a mellow Georgian Manor house set in 30 acres of park and woodland, peacefully situated in the countryside between the Yorkshire Moors and Dales. It offers a tranquil, comfortable environment for courses and workshops or personal non-directed retreats. There are 22 double or twin rooms with en suite facilities. Vegetarian catering. No smoking in the Hall. For brochure and course programme please write or call.

Amadeus Vegetarian Hotel

☑ **Bed & Breakfast**
9 bedspaces in 5 rooms
Amadeus Vegetarian Hotel
115 Franklin Road
Harrogate
North Yorkshire
HG1 5EN
Telephone: 01423 505151
Peaceful Victorian house. Luxurious en suite rooms. Superb vegetarian and vegan food with home-made bread and organic wines. Non-smoking. Only ten minutes walk from the centre of this elegant spa town. Close to

York and the Dales plus the North Yorkshire Moors.

Birchcliffe Centre

☑ **Venue**
62 bedspaces in 16 rooms
Birchcliffe Centre
Birchcliffe Road
Hebden Bridge
West Yorkshire
HX7 8DG
Telephone: 01422 843626
Facsimile: 01422 842424
Scandinavian style conversion gives 15 four-bedded plus one twin en-suite room. Full catering service. Good road and rail links. Peaceful surroundings.

Mountain Hall Centre

☑ **Venue**
☑ **Workshops**
23 bedspaces in 13 rooms
Mountain Hall Centre
Queensbury
West Yorkshire
BD13 1LH
Telephone: 01274 816258
Situated at 1200 feet, with distant vistas, our centre is

Yorkshire & Humberside

acclaimed for quality of food,
accommodation and tuition.
Convenient for towns and
countryside.

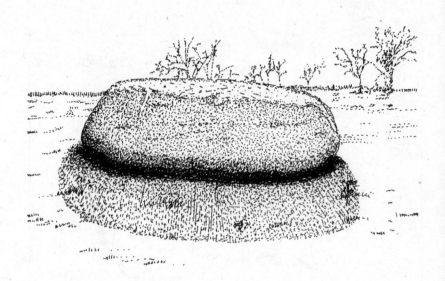

East Anglia

Places to Be

The drawing on the previous page shows the
Growing Stone at Blaxhall, Suffolk

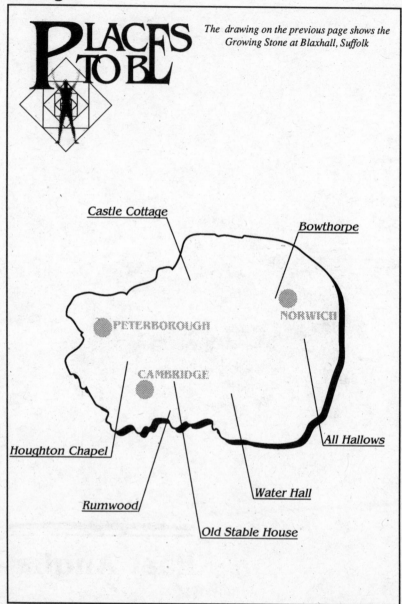

Castle Cottage

Bowthorpe

PETERBOROUGH

NORWICH

CAMBRIDGE

Houghton Chapel

All Hallows

Rumwood

Water Hall

Old Stable House

Houghton Chapel Retreat

☑ **Retreats**
☑ **Venue**
**30 bedspaces in
6 rooms**
*Contact: Sue & Gerry
Feakes*
Houghton Chapel Retreat
Church View, Chapel Lane
Houghton, Huntingdon
Cambridgeshire
PE17 2AY
Telephone: 01480 69376

We offer comfortable modern accommodation, in this riverside village, for groups arranging their own programmes. We have 30 beds in six rooms, lounge, dining room, kitchen, central heating, television/video and table tennis. Children welcome. Brochure available.

Rumwood - Rest & Healing

☑ **Retreats**
☑ **Venue**
☑ **Workshops**
☑ **Bed & Breakfast**
6 bedspaces in 3 rooms
Contact: Mary & Robin Ellis
Rumwood
Cardinal's Green
Horseheath, Cambridgeshire
CB1 6QX
Telephone: 01223 891729
Facsimile: 01223 892596

Amid the peaceful, rolling countryside of south Cambridgeshire, Mary and Robin welcome you into their warm and comfortable cedar-wood home to relax, unwind and "just be" for a while. With spacious sunny rooms, beautiful gardens, a swimming pool and sauna, Reiki Healing, Traditional Thai Massage and Bach Flower Remedies, and a loving atmosphere of caring and sharing, you can find rest, peace and positivity to recharge your energies in *"a little piece of paradise"*. *"Beautiful people in a beautiful place."* Chrissy. *"Lovely to come to this peaceful cocoon. I'm going home rested and refreshed."* Brenda. Weekend courses include the Findhorn Foundation "Game of Transformation", Reiki attunements and seminars, Crystal Healing Workshops and "Creativism" Section 1 of the Avatar Workshops. The vegetarian/vegan food is simply delicious and mealtime conversations are fascinating, fun and inspirational! *"From Devas to Daffodils - the brightest conversation and the best coffee I've ever known!"* Don. Rumwood is only one hour or so from London - by car or train - and less than two hours from Birmingham. To get in touch - and for more details - please give us a ring or drop us a line.

The Old Stable House Centre

- ☑ **Retreats**
- ☑ **Venue**
- ☑ **Workshops**

14 bedspaces in 9 rooms

The Old Stable House Centre
3 Sussex Lodge
Fordham Road
Newmarket
Suffolk
CB8 7AF
Telephone: 01638 667190
Facsimile: 01638 667975

This old stable building was converted in 1989 to create a small retreat and spirituality centre with an attractive, restful environment. While conveniently close to the racing town of Newmarket, the

house is in a green, secluded setting. The nearby gallops provide lots of scope for walking. The centre supports men and women in their personal and spiritual growth by offering a programme of workshops and retreats with an holistic, creation-centred focus. In addition, we welcome individuals who are looking for an informal, friendly environment for time out, reflection or retreat on a self-catering basis. Personal support is available if desired. The facility is available for hire, also on a self-catering basis; however, catering can be arranged if required.

Water Hall Retreat Centre

☑ **Retreats**
☑ **Venue**
☑ **Workshops**
21 bedspaces in 8 rooms
Contact: Karmabandhu
Water Hall Retreat Centre
Daisy Green
Great Ashfield
Bury St Edmunds
Suffolk
IP31 3HT
Telephone: 0181 981 1225
A rural retreat connected with the London Buddhist Centre. Regular introductory retreats run from Friday evening to Sunday afternoon.

Community of All Hallows

☑ **Retreats**
☑ **Venue**
☑ **Workshops**
120 bedspaces
Community of All Hallows
Belsey Bridge Road
Ditchingham
Bungay
Suffolk
NR25 2DT
Telephone: 01986 892749

Retreat/ conference centres and individual guest houses. Extensive facilities both catered and self catering.

Bowthorpe Community Trust

☑ **Retreats**
☑ **Bed & Breakfast**
3 bedspaces in 2 rooms
1 St Michael's Cottages
Bowthorpe Hall Road
Bowthorpe
Norwich
NR5 9AA
Telephone: 01603 746380

East Anglia

Saint Michael's Cottage offers short stay accommodation for those seeking rest, renewal or a short break. One single and one double bedroom. Telephone for a brochure.

Castle Cottage

☑ **Retreats**
☑ **Workshops**
☑ **Bed & Breakfast**
3 bedspaces in 2 rooms
Castle Cottage
Castle Square
Castle Acre
Norfolk
PE32 2AJ
Telephone: 01760 755888
Facsimile: 01760 755888

Specialist Macrobiotic B&B and evening meals. Historic rural village setting. Cooking courses; counselling/healing meditation group. Phone for a free brochure. Nigel and Jackie Walker also run "Vegiventures" - see *Outside the UK* section.

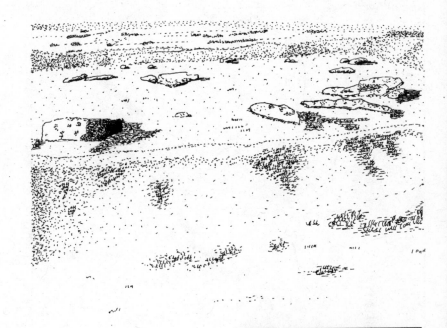

East
Midlands

Places to Be

The drawing on the previous page shows the stone circle at Arbor Low in Derbyshire

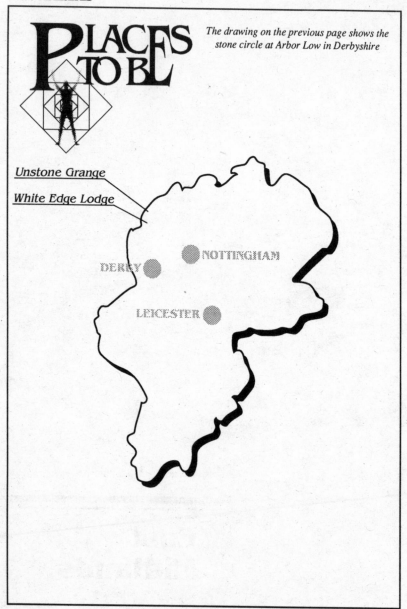

Unstone Grange

White Edge Lodge

DERBY

NOTTINGHAM

LEICESTER

White Edge Lodge

☑ **Retreats**
☑ **Venue**
☑ **Workshops**
15 bedspaces in 3 rooms
Contact: John Wragg or Carl Munson
White Edge Lodge
Longshaw Estate
Derbyshire
S11 7TZ
Telephone: 01742 670308
Facsimile: 01740 665719
Eighteenth Century lodge with breath-taking views in the Peak National Park. Managed by the Flame Foundation - an educational charity.

Unstone Grange

☑ **Retreats**
☑ **Venue**
☑ **Workshops**
40 bedspaces in 10 rooms
Unstone Grange Trust
Unstone Grange
Crow Lane
Unstone
Derbyshire
S18 5AL
Telephone: 01246 412344

Set in the splendour of Derbyshire's countryside, the atmosphere at Unstone Grange attracts those seeking a wider experience of life.

WWOOF

Joining WWOOF opens up a whole new world of opportunities as well as places where you can find out about different ways of being and doing.

WWOOF is an exchange. In return for work on organic farms, gardens and smallholdings (full time and quite hard!) "WWOOFers" receive meals, accommodation and, if necessary, transport to and from the local station.

How it operates

Details of places throughout the UK needing help each weekend are listed in the newsletter, which is sent to members every two months.

Members can then make bookings for the weekends or days of their choice and, if a place is available, will receive full details including travel information.

The newsletter also gives details of events, developments, training and job opportunities in the organic movement and includes members' contributions and advertisements.

For further information write to WWOOF at:
19 Bradford Road
Lewes
Sussex
BN7 1RB

WWOOF
Working for Organic Growers

Aims

- to get first hand experience of organic farming and growing
- to get into the countryside
- to help the organic movement which is labour intensive and does not rely on artificial fertilizers for fertility or persistent poisons for pest control
- to make contact with other people in the organic movement

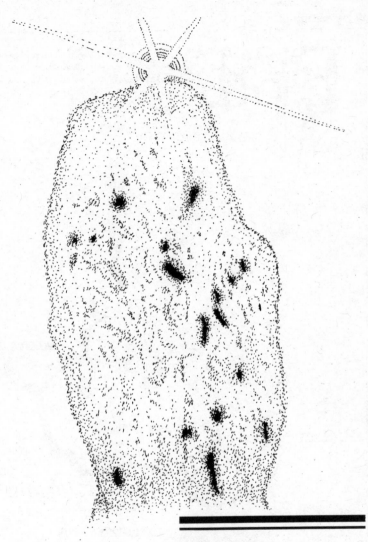

**West
Midlands**

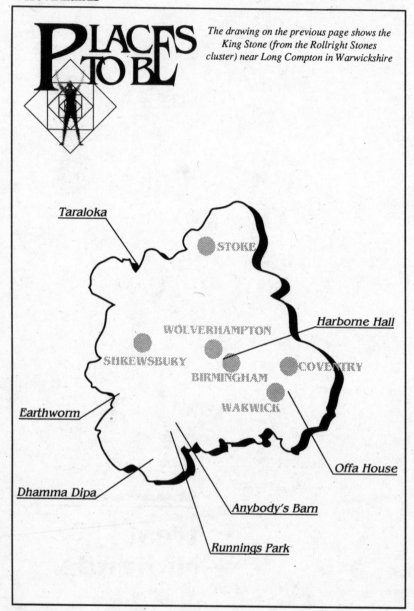

Places to Be

The drawing on the previous page shows the King Stone (from the Rollright Stones cluster) near Long Compton in Warwickshire

Taraloka

STOKE

Harborne Hall

WOLVERHAMPTON

SHREWSBURY

BIRMINGHAM

COVENTRY

Earthworm

WARWICK

Offa House

Dhamma Dipa

Anybody's Barn

Runnings Park

Harborne Hall

☑ **Venue**
100 bedspaces in 74 rooms
Voluntary Service Overseas
Harborne Hall
Old Church Road
Harborne
Birmingham
B17 0BE
Telephone: 0121 428 3249

A delightful residential training centre set in seven acres of grounds. Nine training rooms available at very competitive rates. All diets catered for - vegetarian food is our speciality.

Offa House

☑ **Retreats**
☑ **Venue**
☑ **Workshops**
☑ **Bed & Breakfast**
33 bedspaces in 26 rooms
Offa House
Offchurch
Leamington Spa
Warwickshire
CV33 9AS
Telephone: 01926 423309
Facsimile: 01926 330350

The Coventry Diocese Retreat and Conference Centre. A Georgian house in rural Warwickshire. Retreats for groups and individuals. Good conference facilities.

Anybody's Barn

☑ **Venue**
20 bedspaces in 5 rooms
Contact: Eve Spence or Lynda Medwell
Anybody's Barn
Birchwood Hall
Storridge
Malvern
Worcestershire
WR13 5EZ
Telephone: 01886 884635

Anybody's Barn is a charity offering residential accommodation for groups and organisations on low budgets and who have few opportunities to stay in a beautiful rural retreat. Social Services, charities or support groups are most welcome. Accommodation consists of a kitchen/dining room, meeting room, workshop and dormitory accommodation.

Runnings Park

- ☑ **Retreats**
- ☑ **Venue**
- ☑ **Workshops**
- ☑ **Bed & Breakfast**

28 bedspaces in 22 rooms

Contact: Lorraine Stephens
Pegasus Foundation
Runnings Park
Croft Bank
West Malvern
Worcestershire
WR14 4BP
Telephone: 01684 573868
Facsimile: 01684 892047

Runnings Park is a centre for health, healing and self-development. A full list of all courses and workshops is available. Phone the above number during office hours.

Dhamma Dīpa

- ☑ **Retreats**
- ☑ **Workshops**

60 bedspaces in 24 rooms

Vipassana Trust
Dhamma Dīpa
Harewood End
Hereford
HR2 8NG
Telephone: 01989 730234
Facsimile: 01989 730450

At Dhamma Dīpa we offer courses in Vipassana Meditation as taught by S N Goenka. Vipassana is one of India's most ancient techniques of meditation, taught by the Buddha 2500 years ago. It is a practical method of self-observation that enables one to dissolve mental tensions and develop greater balance of mind. The practice is acceptable to people of all faiths and to those with no particular faith. It helps all to lead a happier and more harmonious life. The technique is taught at ten-day residential courses, organised by the UK Vipassana Trust, which exists solely for the purpose of offering meditation courses and is not connected with any sect or religious organisation. The courses are financed entirely by voluntary donations. Set in 22 acres in the gently rolling hills of south Herefordshire, Dhamma Dīpa offers a calm and peaceful environment amidst beautiful surroundings. All sincere people are welcome to join a Vipassana course to see for themselves how the technique works and to measure the benefits. Please write or phone for further information.

Earthworm

☑ **Venue**
☑ **Workshops**
12 bedspaces in 4 rooms
Contact: any Earthworm Housing Co-op member
Wheatstone
Dark Lane
Leintwardine
Shropshire
SY7 0LH
Telephone: 01547 3 461

Camping field (approximately 100 capacity) with covered catering/dining area. Three fire areas, running water, compost toilets, large cooker. A few indoor rooms/ workshops. Work commenced August 1994 to develop further indoor facilities. We improve the events facilities every year with any profit made from the previous season; aim to remain the best value for money "green" venue and accessible to those on low incomes. Act mainly as hosts but also run several small events ourselves. Seven acres with interesting house and outbuildings, Welsh Border of The Marches. Pretty, rural, close to village facilities. Accessible by public transport; 1.5 hours drive from Birmingham; 2 hours Bristol; 2.5 hours Manchester. Many attractive features: organic gardens, orchard, mature trees; many people find it a very spiritual place. Managed by a small co-operative community along ecological, organic, permacultural principles. Children welcome - suits outdoor fans.

Ideal for practical crafts, horticulture, green gatherings and celebrations, permaculture, building and renovation. May allow special rates or free accommodation to course organisers in return for practical work/ skills/ tuition to residents. Rarely cook for large events but have contact/ arrangements with several catering co-ops. Prefer catering to be at least vegetarian. Site visit welcome by advance arrangement. Please contact us in writing with details/ requirements.

Taraloka Buddhist Retreat Centre for Women

☑ **Retreats**
☑ **Workshops**
24 bedspaces in 5 rooms
Contact: The Secretary
Taraloka Buddhist Retreat Centre for Women
Cornhill Farm
Bettisfield
Whitchurch
Shropshire
SY13 2LD
Telephone: 01948 710646
Electronic mail:
taraloka@100073,3502

We run retreats, teaching meditation and Buddhism. Open to all women. Vegetarian/vegan food. Country walks, peace, friendship, fun!

If you discover a venue that's not listed in this edition of *Places to BE* then let us know ... fill in the reply-paid card at the back of the book and send it off straight away!

Wales

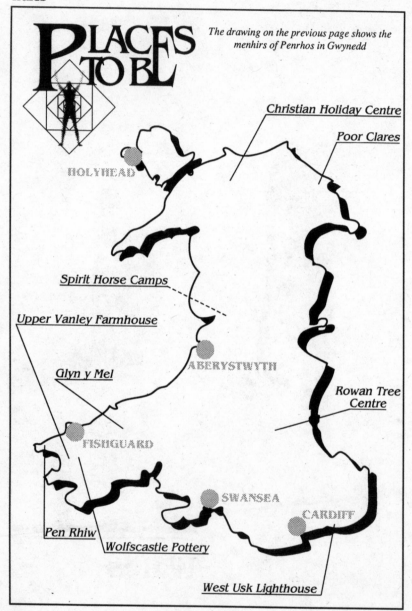

Places to Be

The drawing on the previous page shows the
menhirs of Penrhos in Gwynedd

Christian Holiday Centre

Poor Clares

HOLYHEAD

Spirit Horse Camps

Upper Vanley Farmhouse

Glyn y Mel

ABERYSTWYTH

Rowan Tree
Centre

FISHGUARD

SWANSEA

CARDIFF

Pen Rhiw

Wolfscastle Pottery

West Usk Lighthouse

Poor Clares

☑ **Retreats**
6 bedspaces in 6 rooms
Poor Clares
Ty Mam Duw
Hawarden
Clwyd
CH5 3EN
Telephone: 01244 531029
We are a community of religious Roman Catholic women leading a life of prayer. Midday meal provided; self catering arranged.

Christian Retreat, Conference & Holiday Centre

☑ **Retreats**
☑ **Venue**
☑ **Workshops**
☑ **Bed & Breakfast**
14 bedspaces in 7 rooms
Contact: Rev John Farrimond
Christian Retreat/ Holiday Centre
Pencraig Arthur
Llanddoged
Llanrwst
Gwynedd
LL26 0DZ
Telephone: 01492 640959
A converted farmhouse in a very quiet rural setting near Snowdonia. John (a retired Methodist minister) and Kath offer private or individually-guided retreats; Enneagram teaching; and "Rekindle"

Weekends for members of the caring professions. Quiet holidays with B&B, half or full board, or self-catering.

The Rowan Tree Centre

☑ **Retreats**
☑ **Workshops**
13 bedspaces in 7 rooms
Contact: Mary Lewis
The Rowan Tree Centre
The Skreen
Erwood
Builth Wells
Powys
LD2 3SJ
Telephone: 01982 560210
The Rowan Tree is a centre for the practice and study of an open, creative and contemplative theology and spirituality that is rooted in and committed to the Christian tradition, whilst exploring new dimensions of faith.

Spirit Horse Camps

☑ **Retreats**
☑ **Venue**
☑ **Workshops**
80 bedspaces in 13 tents
Contact: Erika or Shivam
19 Holmwood Gardens
London
N3 3NS
Telephone: 0181 346 3660

Wales

Spirit Horse Camps hosts spiritual retreats, performing arts and shamanic personal growth events camped out in wildest Wales (and Ireland) in tribal tents and traditional nomadic structures. Main focus directed towards Tibetan, Native American and Celtic "sacred view": sweatlodge, meditation, ceremony, male and female initiation, authentic communication, respect for the 'wild' and a spiritual ecological harmony. Yearly programme includes Nyingma Buddhist Lama Ngakpa Chogyar Rinpoche; Shamanic Contemplation and Enlightenment Intensive with Shivam O'Brien; Sacred Sexuality with the Spirit Horse Team; and drumming, singing, dancing and storytelling with a variety of accomplished facilitators.

Wolfscastle Pottery & Activity Centre

☑ **Retreats**
☑ **Venue**
☑ **Workshops**
8 bedspaces in 5 rooms
Contact: Philip Cunningham
Wolfscastle Pottery
Wolfscastle
Haverfordwest
Pembrokeshire
SA62 5LZ
Telephone: 01437 741609
Facsimile: 01437 741609
Personal growth and stress management using the medium of clay - handbuiling and throwing on the wheel, plus yoga, aromatherapy, coasteering, abseiling and surfing. Warm, caring, friendly atmosphere; delicious organic food; spectacular coastal scenery.

Upper Vanley Farmhouse

☑ **Retreats**
☑ **Venue**
☑ **Workshops**
☑ **Bed & Breakfast**
14 bedspaces in 6 rooms
Contact: Carol Shales
Upper Vanley Farmhouse
Llandewy
Solva
Pembrokeshire
SA62 6LJ
Telephone: 01348 831418
Delightful B&B/Farmhouse close to spectacular Pembrokeshire Coastal Path, islands, baby seals, rare birds. Imaginative cuisine, en suite accommodation. Ideal workshop venue with outdoor pursuits offered as an additional activity. Occasional Alexander Technique

Holidays. House available for workshop hire or for individuals to stay.

Glyn y Mel

☑ **Retreats**
☑ **Bed & Breakfast**
4 bedspaces in 2 rooms
Contact: Mr & Mrs Bryant
Glyn y Mel
Capel Iwan
Newcastle Emlyn
Dyfed
SA38 9NG
Telephone: 01559 371287

Tranquility Breaks. Offering organic food and complementary therapies. Relax in our one acre conservation garden with panoramic views over the Preseli Hills. Non-smoking establishment. B&B also available. Telephone for a brochure.

Pen Rhiw

☑ **Venue**
33 bedspaces in 20 rooms
Contact: Steve or Lis Cousens
Pen Rhiw
St David's
Pembrokeshire
SA62 6PG
Telephone: 01437 721821

Our purpose at Pen Rhiw is to provide a comfortable residential centre for groups, in a powerful and beautiful setting, with a friendly and welcoming atmosphere. The house itself is wonderful; there are twenty bedrooms giving up to thirty-three places; almost all have washbasins, there is central heating throughout and plenty of bathrooms and loos. The main group room is 50 x 16 ft, light and airy and with tremendous views of open countryside. There is a range of other spaces. We are situated just outside St David's in the Pembrokeshire Coast National Park, an area of outstanding beauty with spectacular beaches and cliffs. Our vegetarian wholefood (much of the green veg grown in our organic garden) is delicious, plentiful and constantly praised. What people who come here (again and again) say is that they really

appreciate the way that we make groups feel at home and safely relaxed and that we are around to meet people's needs without intruding into what the group is doing.

West Usk Lighthouse

☑ **Venue**
☑ **Workshops**
☑ **Bed & Breakfast**
10 bedspaces in 6 rooms

Contact: Frank & Danielle Sheahan
West Usk Lighthouse
Lighthouse Road
St Brides
Wentloog Newport
Gwent
NP1 9SF
Telephone: 01633 810126/815860
Facsimile: 01633 815582

Situated between Newport and Cardiff, the West Usk is a real lighthouse, built in 1821 (now Grade II listed) to a unique design in order to house two families of lighthouse keepers. The lighthouse overlooks the Bristol Channel and the Severn Estuary as well as the Welsh hills and valleys. All rooms are

wedge-shaped, with a slate bedded entrance hall which leads to an internal collective well. The Lighthouse can sleep ten and has workshop facilities in an outbuilding. Couples, singles and children are most welcome. The atmosphere is peaceful and relaxing so it is an ideal place to unwind - either through the use of the flotation tank combined with an aromatherapy massage - or simply letting go. The Lighthouse is on crossing leys and has a certain je ne sais quoi about it. For the romantics there is a waterbed and four-poster bed (en suite rooms). Coastal walks (along deserted sea wall) and breathing fresh air is quite an inviting proposition to any city-dweller! Log fire in lounge in the winter, workshops on a regular basis: resident esoteric astrologer and tarot consultant and much more. Vegans and vegetarians catered for - non smoking establishment. From £20 B&B. Full tariff on request.

South West
England

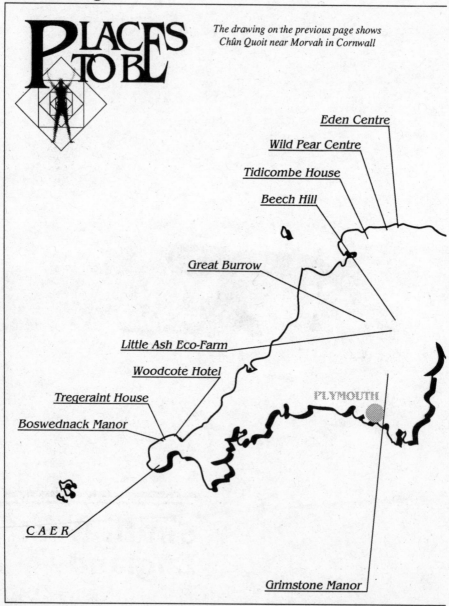

*The drawing on the previous page shows
Chûn Quoit near Morvah in Cornwall*

Eden Centre

Wild Pear Centre

Tidicombe House

Beech Hill

Great Burrow

Little Ash Eco-Farm

Woodcote Hotel

Tregeraint House

Boswednack Manor

PLYMOUTH

CAER

Grimstone Manor

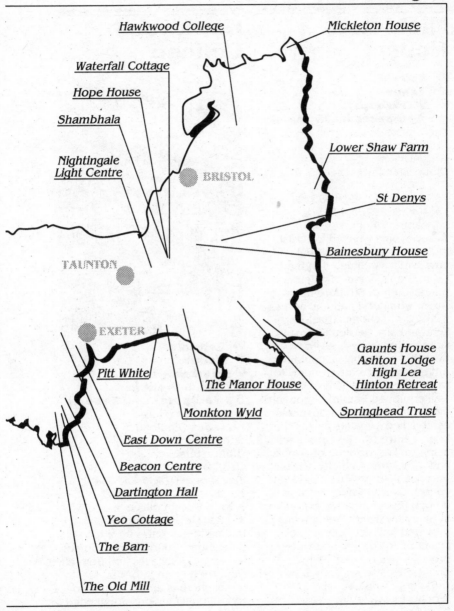

Hawkwood College

Mickleton House

Waterfall Cottage

Hope House

Shambhala

Nightingale
Light Centre

BRISTOL

Lower Shaw Farm

St Denys

Bainesbury House

TAUNTON

EXETER

Gaunts House
Ashton Lodge
High Lea
Hinton Retreat

Pitt White

The Manor House

Springhead Trust

Monkton Wyld

East Down Centre

Beacon Centre

Dartington Hall

Yeo Cottage

The Barn

The Old Mill

Mickleton House

☑ **Retreats**
☑ **Venue**
☑ **Workshops**
50 bedspaces in 25 rooms
The Emissaries
Mickleton House
Mickleton
Gloucestershire
GL55 6RY
Telephone: 01386 438251
Facsimile: 01386 438118

A centre for courses, workshops or events which may assist individuals in their spiritual and creative lives. Situated in the Cotswold village of Mickleton, 8 miles south of Stratford-upon-Avon, with good national access from all directions. Spacious, light and airy Garden Room suitable for many uses - a beautiful and magical container built to allow creative energy to work and move. Light, quiet and well-equipped Seminar Room also available. Mickleton House was established 14 years ago as the heart centre of 'The Emissaries', a spiritual association of people and a registered charity, whose purpose is to provide a place in consciousness where Spirit may be real and generative expression in everyday living. Full catering provided and accommodation available in conjunction with programmes offered. The Emissaries also stage their own workshops and courses. Brochures available.

Hawkwood College

☑ **Retreats**
☑ **Venue**
☑ **Workshops**
☑ **Bed & Breakfast**
52 bedspaces in 32 rooms
Hawkwood College
Painswick Old Road
Stroud
Gloucestershire
GL6 7QW
Telephone: 01453 759034
Facsimile: 01453 764607

Hawkwood College, a Registered Charity, is an independent centre for adult education. It offers short courses to people of all ages and from all walks of life. An informal atmosphere is aimed at and no formal qualifications are needed to participate. Over and above courses which offer experience in music, science, arts and crafts, Hawkwood seeks to foster - through a variety of courses and seminars - ways and means to a spiritual foundation of life to counterbalance the materialistic values which dominate most fields of human activity today. There is particular reference to the work of Rudolf Steiner. Hawkwood, an early 19th Century manor house built on an ancient site, is surrounded by its own extensive grounds. Situated at the head of a small Cotswold valley with a panoramic view down the Severn Vale it provides a beautiful and peaceful setting for an Adult Education Centre.

St Denys Retreat Centre

☑ **Retreats**
☑ **Venue**
☑ **Workshops**
28 bedspaces in 22 rooms
St Denys Retreat Centre
2 Church Street
Warminster
Wiltshire
BA12 8PG
Telephone: 01985 214824
Ground floor room available for disabled people (wheelchair access). Not suitable for children.

Lower Shaw Farm

☑ **Retreats**
☑ **Venue**
☑ **Workshops**
40 bedspaces in 15 rooms
Contact: Matt Holland
Lower Shaw Farm
Old Shaw Lane
Shaw
Swindon
Wiltshire
SN5 9PJ
Telephone: 01793 771080
Formerly a North Wiltshire dairy farm, Lower Shaw is now a thriving community and residential centre. Since the late 1970s it has been running courses in 'alternatives' and hiring out its facilities to groups and organisations. It has a wealth of experience in catering for all needs. It has basic but homely accommodation; large meeting rooms; and a rustic but civilised feel. Groups and individuals say that its strength lies in enabling and creating a good communal

feeling of living, working and playing together. It is readily accessible by rail or motorway and is only a few miles from Avebury stones and the Ridgeway. It has some animals, a big garden and lots going on. It can be as quiet or as buzzing as you like. Full programme of courses and hire charge details always available. We welcome telephone enquiries.

Gaunts House

☑ **Retreats**
☑ **Venue**
☑ **Workshops**
☑ **Bed & Breakfast**
120 bedspaces in 45 rooms
Contact: Paul Sax
Gaunts House
Wimborne
Dorset
BH21 4JQ
Telephone: 01202 841522
Facsimile: 01202 841959

Gaunts House is the principal centre of the 2,000 acre Gaunts Estate, dedicated to being a safe and supportive learning environment for personal growth and human evolution. A comfortable stately home set in beautiful Dorset parkland with miles of country walks, run by an empathetic resident community. Elegant workshop space, barn theatre, esoteric book and audio-visual library, tennis, squash and swimming. We provide excellent vegetarian catering at all our centres. Gaunts House is also home of the Glyn Foundation which runs a full programme of 'life-enhancement' courses, write or call for a free brochure.

Ashton Lodge

☑ **Venue**
☑ **Workshops**
37 bedspaces in 18 rooms
Ashton Lodge
care of Gaunts House

Set on a hill with views over the Allen Valley, Ashton Lodge is an ideal course venue for groups of up to 40 persons. Part of the Gaunts Estate, Ashton Lodge is available for self-catering groups or we can supply full board and all necessary support.

High Lea

☑ **Venue**
☑ **Workshops**
80 bedspaces in 14 rooms
High Lea
care of Gaunts House

High Lea is an attractive centre in the heart of rural Dorset.

Formerly a progressive school it consists of both farmhouse and school buildings. It is ideal for residential youth groups and for religious retreats. The large gym, in particular, is suitable as workshop or ritual space. Accommodation is both dormitory and shared, self-catering or catered.

Hinton House

☑ **Retreats**
10 bedspaces in 8 rooms
Hinton House
care of Gaunts House

Hinton is a retreat house designed to accommodate those in need of a peaceful countryside haven. It has log fires, bread ovens, low ceilings and miles of walks on the Gaunts Estate. Stays can be from three days to one month. Guests cook and clean for themselves.

Monkton Wyld Court

☑ **Retreats**
☑ **Venue**
☑ **Workshops**
☑ **Bed & Breakfast**
34 bedspaces in 11 rooms
Monkton Wyld Court
Charmouth
Bridport
Dorset
DT6 6DQ
Telephone: 01297 560342

Our Centre for Holistic Education offers a wealth of inspirational courses in the beauty and tranquility of our eleven acre estate, three miles from the sea.

Pitt White

☑ **Retreats**
☑ **Venue**
☑ **Workshops**
☑ **Bed & Breakfast**
18 bedspaces in 9 rooms
Pitt White
Mill Lane
Uplyme
Lyme Regis
Dorset
DT2 3TZ
Telephone: 01297 442094

Pitt White Licensed Guest House (ETB 3 Crowns, Commended). En suite rooms. Vegetarian/wholefoods. Famous bamboo and woodland gardens. Sauna. Flotation tank. Jaccuzzi. Workshops. Phone for a brochure.

The Manor House

- ☑ **Retreats**
- ☑ **Venue**
- ☑ **Workshops**
- ☑ **Bed & Breakfast**

6 bedspaces in 3 rooms
The Manor House
North Street
Beaminster
Dorset
DT8 3DZ
Telephone: 01308 862311
Facsimile: 01308 862311

This elegant house provides a special place for guests to relax in the peace and quiet of the Dorset countryside.

Springhead Trust

- ☑ **Retreats**
- ☑ **Venue**
- ☑ **Workshops**

39 bedspaces in 8 rooms
Contact: Peter Hood
Springhead Trust
Fontmell Magna
Shaftesbury
Dorset
SP7 0NU
Telephone: 01747 811853
Facsimile: 01747 811853

Environment education, inner/outer ecology, folk dance, drama. All ages welcome to this old mill in beautiful gardens beside the springs and lake in rural Dorset.

Bainesbury House

- ☑ **Retreats**
- ☑ **Venue**

17 bedspaces in 4 rooms
Bainesbury House
Downside Abbey
Stratton on the Fosse
Bath
Avon
BA3 4RH
Telephone: 01761 232295
Facsimile: 01761 232973

Bainesbury House is in the grounds of the Benedictine monastery at Downside in Somerset. It is suitable for groups of up to 17 persons (more with camp beds) who want a quiet, informal, homely, low-cost, self-catering venue with the possible use of: school facilities for swimming and most sports; walks and space; attendance at Abbey services; spiritual talks and advice (if required); prayer and a prayerful place.

Shambhala Healing Centre

☑ **Retreats**
☑ **Venue**
☑ **Workshops**
☑ **Bed & Breakfast**
10 bedspaces in 5 rooms
Contact: Serahsee
Shambhala Healing Centre
Glastonbury
Somerset
BA6 8BH
Telephone: 01458 831797/833081
Facsimile: 01458 834751

We welcome you to our Healing Centre to enjoy our wood-burning sauna, large seven-seater jacuzzi set in a conservatory full of exotic plants, Aromatherapy massage, Shiatsu massage, and in-depth counselling. We are a team of dedicated, sensitive, loving healers and would especially recommend one of our *Intensive 3-Day Healing Breaks*, when you'll be pampered and cared for completely. Staying in the Shambhala Guest House is an intense and loving experience and you have the choice of an Egyptian, Tibetan or Chinese bedroom. Please book well in advance! We also cook wonderful vegetarian lunches and suppers. Shambhala is a sacred site and we have a beautiful seven-pointed Crystal Star which marks the Heart of the Heart. People come from all over the world to visit our centre and we know you will enjoy it and receive great benefit from your visit. Sited on the wooded slopes of the Tor, we look over the magnificent Vale of Avalon and you can enjoy our gardens, with pond and waterfall, and our flock of white doves. Inspiring, welcoming, restful and fun!

Waterfall Cottage Healing Centre

☑ **Workshops**
☑ **Bed & Breakfast**
6 bedspaces in 4 rooms
Waterfall Cottage Healing Centre
20 Old Wells Road
Glastonbury
Somerset
BA6 8ED
Telephone: 01458 831707

Bed and Breakfast in a beautiful 17th Century cottage radiating peace and harmony. Country walks from the door. Ancient sites cloaked in myth and legend - maps and guides available. Library of spiritual/healing books available. Use of garden and patio. Therapies - crystal healing; flower oils and essences; regression - gentle, beautiful and nurturing. A place to unwind and recharge. Guided tours of ancient sites on request. Workshops on crystals, colour, inner growth. All diets.

Hope House Healing Sanctuary

☑ **Retreats**
☑ **Workshops**
☑ **Bed & Breakfast**
6 bedspaces in 3 rooms
Hope House Healing Sanctuary
51 Benedict Street
Glastonbury
Somerset
BA6 9DB
Telephone: 01458 834451

Hope House Healing Sanctuary is a unique, inspiring home-from-home and Centre of Light for nurturing, healing holidays, B&B; specialising in Hawaiian Massage and help with self-awareness and spirituality. A wonderful space to gain clarity and renewal and also visit the sacred sites of Glastonbury.

Nightingale Light Centre

☑ **Retreats**
☑ **Venue**
☑ **Workshops**
☑ **Bed & Breakfast**
12 bedspaces in 5 rooms

Nightingale Light Centre
Nightingale Farm
Beer
Aler
Somerset
TA10 0QX
Telephone: 01458 253401

Our purpose is to create a playground of love, healing, inspiration, peace and rejuvenation on all levels (physical, mental, emotional, spiritual, etheric and planetary). We offer individual sessions in cranial-sacral therapy, body harmony, gem/crystal remedies, counselling, core therapy, and rebirthing. We run groups for women on earth energies. Mixed groups on body work and personal empowerment.

Beech Hill Community

☑ **Retreats**
☑ **Venue**
☑ **Workshops**
☑ **Bed & Breakfast**
20 bedspaces in 6 rooms
Contact: Dawn or Abi
Beech Hill Community
Morchard Bishop
near Crediton
Devon
EX17 6RF
Telephone: 01363 877228

Beech Hill is set in seven acres of grounds and gardens in a quiet, rural location midway between Dartmoor and Exmoor. Our newly converted garden house offers comfortable, small-

dormitory accommodation; plus kitchen and lounge area with wood-burning stove. Large rooms available with good workspace for dance, drumming, t'ai chi etc. We are a friendly community able to provide superb wholefood catering. Alternatively courses can be self catered. An outdoor swimming pool is available in summer months. Opening Autumn 1995.

Little Ash Eco-Farm

☑ **Retreats**
☑ **Venue**
☑ **Workshops**
☑ **Bed & Breakfast**
5 bedspaces in 3 rooms
Little Ash Eco-Farm
Throwleigh
Okehampton
Devon
EX20 2HY
Telephone: 01647 231394
Electronic mail:
mkileywo@ac.exeter.uk
Experience ecological living. Wind power, own water, food. Courses: eco-agriculture, horses (working and riding), animal behaviour and welfare. Phone first. Numbers can be larger with camping.

Great Burrow

☑ **Retreats**
2 bedspaces in 1 room
Contact: Marianne & Michael Brookman
Great Burrow
Bratton Clovelly
Okehampton
Devon
EX20 4JJ
Telephone: 01837 871454

Retreat Weekends for one and two people in the peace and comfort of our home, an ancient thatched farmhouse overlooking a vast panorama of Dartmoor, with the opportunity to explore the roots of health/stress problems, introducing a simple way of life beyond dependence upon technique and belief systems. Other professional services available: Herbalism, Healing and Iridology. Vegetarian wholefood par excellence.

Tidicombe House

☑ **Retreats**
☑ **Venue**
☑ **Workshops**
☑ **Bed & Breakfast**
12 bedspaces in 6 rooms
Contact: Cheryl or Edward Thornburgh
Tidicombe House
Arlington
near Barnstaple
Devon
EX31 4SP
Telephone: 01271 850626
Facsimile: 01271 850626

Tidicombe lies peacefully isolated amidst the woods and hills of North Devon. Exmoor and the coast are a short drive and there is horse riding nearby. We offer vegetarian B&B; full board if you can lend a hand; eventually self-catering accommodation for groups/courses *(probably 1996)*. Sorry, no pets or smoking. We are renovating our barns to make craft workshops and creating organic gardens for food, enjoyment and reflection. We are especially interested in creating positive visions for a

changing world - both locally and globally - and welcome visitors' ideas. We plan to hold gatherings to explore these issues, to seed ideas generally and to find our personal ways of taking part in this exciting time of evolutionary leaps. Our base is spiritual, our aim practical. Our interests include arts/crafts, folk music, puppet theatre and permaculture. We also help run North Devon LETS. We need help with building/renovation/gardening. If you have skills/practicality, enthusiasm *and* humour, we can offer periods of accommodation in return for work. But please, no more "heavy baggage"! We want to lighten poor old Gaia, not weigh her down ... We aim to offer Advances, not Retreats - or Escapes!! Please write for more information.

Wild Pear Centre

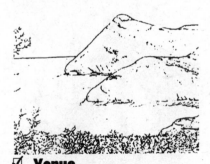

☑ **Venue**
☑ **Workshops**
25 bedspaces in 5 rooms

Wild Pear Centre
King Street
Combe Martin
Devon
EX34 0AG
Telephone: 01271 883086

A centre for personal growth work where Exmoor meets the sea. Residential group space for hire, with or without catering, at very reasonable rates.

The Eden Centre

☑ **Retreats**
☑ **Workshops**
7 bedspaces in 3 rooms
Contact: Jenny Davis
The Eden Centre
Eden House
38 Lee Road
Lynton
Devon
EX35 6BS
Telephone: 01598 53440

The Eden Centre, set in an unspoilt Area of Outstanding Natural Beauty, offers retreats; aromatherapy; reflexology; creative workshops; poetry; photography. A small centre for healing and creative development yet part of a wider vision including the work and impulse of Rudolph Steiner. Brochure available. Also individually priced self-catering.

East Down Centre

☑ **Venue**
16 bedspaces in 4 rooms
Contact: Richard Jones
East Down Centre
Dunsford
Exeter
Devon
EX6 7AL
Telephone: 01647 24546

Peaceful accommodation for small groups or workshops. No sharing with other groups. Self-catering or catered. Sympathetically converted thatched barn set in beautiful country within the Dartmoor National Park.

Devon
EX4 2HE
Telephone: 01392 811203

A residential centre offering a variety of courses/ workshops/ retreats in personal growth and spiritual awakening. We offer catered (vegetarian) or self-catering facilities in two lovely group rooms and comfortable accommodation. Set amid the Devon Hills, we are only a short distance from Dartmoor and the south Devon coast. Therapies also available.

The Beacon Centre

☑ **Retreats**
☑ **Venue**
☑ **Workshops**
☑ **Bed & Breakfast**
30 bedspaces in 11 rooms
Contact: Wendy Webber
The Beacon Centre
Cutteridge Farm
Whitestone
Exeter

Dartington Hall Conference Centre

☑ **Venue**
☑ **Bed & Breakfast**
280 bedspaces in 260 rooms
Contact: Julie Piper
Dartington Hall Conference Centre
Dartington
Totnes
Devon
TQ9 6EL
Telephone: 01803 866051
Facsimile: 01803 868386
Situated in the heart of an 800 acre estate, bounded by the River Dart, yet only two miles from Totnes.

The Barn Retreat Community

☑ **Retreats**
7 bedspaces in 7 rooms
Contact: The Manager
The Barn Retreat Community
Lower Sharpham Barton
Ashprington
Totnes
Devon
TQ9 7DX
Telephone: 01803 732661
A working retreat centre for people with some meditation experience. Based on Buddhist tradition but non-denominational. Stays from 2 weeks to 6 months.

Yeo Cottage

☑ **Retreats**
☑ **Workshops**
☑ **Bed & Breakfast**
6 bedspaces in 3 rooms
Yeo Cottage
Sandwell Lane
Totnes
Devon
TQ9 7LJ
Telephone: 01803 868157
Days or weeks - breaks for peace, relaxation, healing. This thatched cottage in its own grounds with beautiful surroundings is two miles from Totnes. A time to be yourself and unwind. We cater for your needs.

The Old Mill

☑ **Venue**
☑ **Workshops**
14 bedspaces in 9 rooms

Centre for Past Life Healing and
Associated Therapies
The Old Mill
Harbertonford
Totnes
Devon
TQ9 7SW
Telephone: 01803 732349

Set in immaculate six and a half acres of gardens and lawns, with our own stream running through, the Mill is part of our rich heritage having been connected with Devon's wool and later foundry industries until the 1950s. Up until 1993 it was operated as a three star country house hotel. Only three hours by train from London, the Old Mill is a peaceful and secluded venue available for hire for residential workshops - with large lounges, open fires, single, twin and double bedrooms (all en suite). As the Centre for Past Life Healing & Associated Therapies we also run training programmes on Past life Healing, Soul Retrieval, Spirit Rescues, Earthbound Releases, Rebirthing, Between Lives and Birth, Pre and Post Surgery Healing and more. A hot tub can be arranged and we have a good space for a sweat lodge.

Grimstone Manor

☑ **Retreats**
☑ **Venue**
☑ **Workshops**
40 bedspaces in 13 rooms

Grimstone Manor
Yelverton
Devon
PL20 7QY
Telephone: 01822 854358

Grimstone Manor is a residential venue on the edge of Dartmoor. It is a very comfortable house with full central heating, an indoor swimming pool, jacuzzi and sauna. Set in over 20 acres of grounds, it offers each course exclusive use of all the facilities. Food is mainly vegetarian and drinks and snacks are available in the dining room 24 hours a day. The Manor is open to courses all year: it is used regularly for courses in yoga, shamanism, dance, psychotherapy and massage, and also offers a variety of holiday and working breaks.

CAER

☑ **Retreats**
☑ **Venue**
☑ **Workshops**
☑ **Bed & Breakfast**
25 bedspaces in 10 rooms

Contact: Jo May
C A E R
Rosemerryn
Lamorna
Penzance
Cornwall
TR19 6BN
Telephone: 01736 810530
Facsimile: 01736 810906

CAER has been providing residential workshops since 1978. The centre is situated one mile from the sea, on the site of an Iron Age fort, secluded in seven acres of woods, gardens and streams. In the grounds is a 2000 year old underground granite passage containing a unique carving of a God of Healing. The surrounding area has sandy beaches and coves, spectacular coastal walks, quaint harbours, wild moors, lush valleys, and more ancient sites than anywhere else in the United Kingdom. All within a designated Area of Outstanding Natural Beauty.

Tregeraint House

☑ **Venue**
☑ **Bed & Breakfast**
7 bedspaces in 3 rooms

Contact: Sue & John Wilson
Tregeraint House
Zennor
St Ives
Cornwall
TR26 3DB
Telephone: 01736 797061
Facsimile: 01736 797061

A roomy traditional granite cottage in a magnificent situation overlooking sea and hills. Warm, friendly place. All diets catered for.

Woodcote Hotel

☑ **Bed & Breakfast**
14 bedspaces in 6 rooms
Woodcote Hotel
The Saltings
Lelant
St Ives
Cornwall
TR26 3DL
Telephone: 01736 753147

Standing in its own grounds, overlooking a beautiful tidal estuary and bird sanctuary - Britain's oldest vegetarian hotel awaits your custom.

Boswednack Manor

☑ **Retreats**
☑ **Workshops**
☑ **Bed & Breakfast**
10 bedspaces in 5 rooms

Contact: Dr Elizabeth Gynn
Boswednack Manor
Zennor
St Ives
Cornwall
TR26 3DP
Telephone: 01736 794183

Peaceful guesthouse in wildest Cornwall overlooking the sea and moors. Organic garden. Meditation room. Guided wildlife walks, birdwatching and wildflower weeks. Bed and Breakfast, vegetarian evening meals. No smoking throughout. Self catering cottage also available.

South East
England

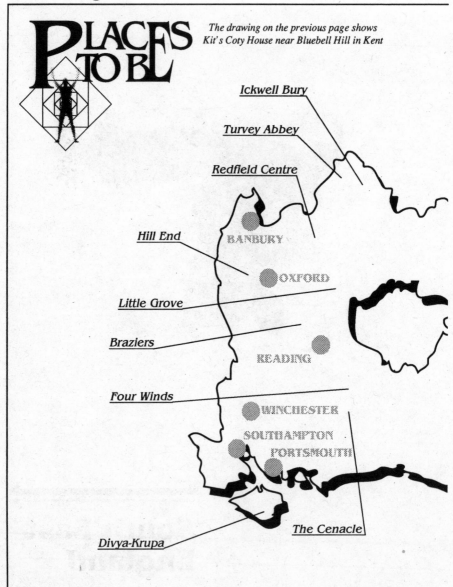

Places to BE

The drawing on the previous page shows
Kit's Coty House near Bluebell Hill in Kent

Ickwell Bury

Turvey Abbey

Redfield Centre

Hill End

BANBURY

OXFORD

Little Grove

Braziers

READING

Four Winds

WINCHESTER

SOUTHAMPTON

PORTSMOUTH

The Cenacle

Divya-Krupa

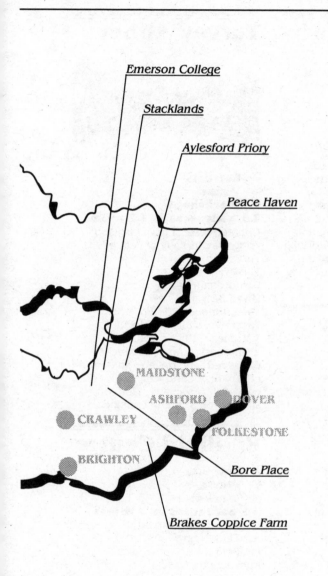

Emerson College

Stacklands

Aylesford Priory

Peace Haven

MAIDSTONE

ASHFORD   DOVER

CRAWLEY   FOLKESTONE

BRIGHTON

Bore Place

Brakes Coppice Farm

Peace Haven

☑ **Retreats**
4 bedspaces in 3 rooms
Contact: Hazell
Peace Haven
30 Church Road
Hadleigh
Essex
SS7 2DQ
Telephone: 01702 554418

This centre of light offers loving support and guidance for those seeking to transform the problems and confusion of life into peace, harmony, love and joy. We provide very comfortable, spacious accommodation and wholesome food for mind, body and spirit.

Ickwell Bury

☑ **Retreats**
☑ **Venue**
☑ **Workshops**
40 bedspaces in 17 rooms
Yoga for Health Foundation
Ickwell Bury
Biggleswade
Bedfordshire
SG18 9EF
Telephone: 01767 627271

Residential yoga centre specialising in teaching people with physical disability and chronic illness. Teacher training courses available.

Turvey Abbey

☑ **Retreats**
☑ **Venue**
☑ **Workshops**
16 bedspaces in 13 rooms
Contact: Sister Lucy M Brydon
Priory of Our Lady of Peace
Turvey Abbey
Turvey
Bedfordshire
MK43 8DE
Telephone: 01234 881432
Facsimile: 01234 881538

Roman Catholic double monastery (Benedictine) offers retreats: private; guided, group; residential; day courses; ecumenical ministry. Thirteen single rooms, home cooking.

Redfield Centre

☑ **Retreats**
☑ **Venue**
☑ **Workshops**
16 bedspaces in 5 rooms
Contact: Chris Watson
Redfield Centre
Redfield
Buckingham Road
Winslow
Buckinghamshire
MK18 3LZ

Little Grove

Telephone: 01296 714983
Facsimile: 01296 714983
Electronic mail:
redfield@gn.apc.org

Accommodation for groups in a peaceful setting halfway between London and Birmingham and convenient for Oxford, Northampton, Milton Keynes and Luton. Residential facilities are located in a self-contained cottage away from the Main House which is occupied by the Redfield Community. 16 people can be accommodated but we have had larger groups by using mattresses on the floor; outlying B&Bs; and (in Summer) camping. Seventeen acre estate includes woodland and tennis court. Groups are usually self-contained but there are possibilities for participating in tasks with members of the Community. Various large meeting spaces available. Special diets catered for within a vegetarian kitchen (self-catering is an option). Groups using the Centre have included: Permaculture designers; Buddhist retreatants; a Socialist choir; and gay men.

☑ **Retreats**
☑ **Venue**
☑ **Workshops**
18 bedspaces in 4 rooms
Contact: Janice Gray or Alan Dale
Little Grove
Grove Lane
Chesham, Buckinghamshire
HP5 3QQ
Telephone: 01494 782720
Facsimile: 01494 776066

A venue in the country near the city. Long established and popular with all kinds of groups. Quiet, beautiful grounds surrounded by farmland. Large airy meeting room and other spaces available, with all visual aids. Excellent catering or.DIY if preferred. Sauna

Hill End

V isualise an organically farmed nature reserve on a sunny hillside outside Oxford with rural outlook to the Downs, Chilterns and the local reservoir. Set aside for children in 1926, Hill End still offers inexpensive, simple, flexible, self-catering facilities for non-profit making, environmental, youth and school groups from 15 to 175. Sixty-five acres of beautiful unspoiled land; camping; swimming pool; barn; disabled facilities (including laundry); wild garden; permaculture field studies; lecture rooms. Local caterers if required. Excellent road/rail access. All buildings are let on a sole-user basis and are scattered to offer a sense of peace. Badgers, foxes and deer share our place and we are a Site of Special Scientific Interest. Work parties welcome, taught courses to your requirements by arrangement.

Braziers Park

☑ **Venue**
☑ **Workshops**
179 bedspaces in 26 rooms
Hill End Residential & Field
Studies Centre
Eynsham Road
Farmoor
Oxford
OX2 9NJ
Telephone: 01865 863510

☑ **Retreats**
☑ **Venue**
☑ **Workshops**
19 bedspaces in 13 rooms
Braziers Adult College
Braziers Park
Ipsden
Wallingford
Oxfordshire
OX10 6AN
Telephone: 01491 680221
Residential college in 17th
Century listed building - run
by a small resident community
with voluntary help from tutors
and overseas students. Courses
offered in Arts and Crafts; Social
Sciences and Philosophy.
Informal atmosphere. Visitors of
all ages and persuasions
welcome.

Four Winds Centre

☑ **Retreats**
☑ **Venue**
☑ **Workshops**
32 bedspaces in 9 rooms
Four Winds Centre
High Thicket Road
Dockenfield
near Farnham
Surrey
GU10 4HB
Telephone: 01252 793990
Facsimile: 01252 793990
A residential transpersonal
centre in a secluded forest
setting 45 miles from London.
Available for groups up to 32
people with option of vegetarian
catering. We also run summer

and winter programmes, and
individual retreats can be
arranged midweek.

The Cenacle

☑ **Retreats**
☑ **Workshops**
39 bedspaces in 30 rooms
Contact: Retreat Secretary
The Cenacle
Grayshott
Hindhead
Surrey
GU26 6DN
Telephone: 01428 604412
This retreat centre offers
retreats, workshops in human
development and spirituality, and
opportunities for quiet days and
spiritual direction.

Divya-Krupa

☑ **Bed & Breakfast**
5 bedspaces in 3 rooms
Authentic Vegan and Vegetarian
Bed & Breakfast
"Divya-Krupa"
Kemming Road
Whitwell
Isle of Wight
PO38 2QT
Telephone: 01983 731279
The only exclusive
vegan/vegetarian B&B on the
Isle of Wight. Peaceful Home of
vegetarian/vegan owners in
picturesque valley village.
Evening meals. Send a stamped
addressed envelope for a
brochure.

Brakes Coppice Farm

☑ **Retreats**
☑ **Bed & Breakfast**
5 bedspaces in 3 rooms
Contact: Fay Ramsden
Brakes Coppice Farm
Telham Lane
Battle
East Sussex
TN33 0SJ
Telephone: 01424 830347
Facsimile: 01424 830347
Specialise in holidays for the elderly. We can look after a dependent relative and give you a well earned break. See the display advertisement or ring Fay to discuss your needs.

Emerson College

☑ **Retreats**
☑ **Venue**
☑ **Workshops**
140 bedspaces in 140 rooms
Emerson College
Forest Row
East Sussex
RH18 5JX
Telephone: 01342 822238
Facsimile: 01342 826055
Emerson College is an adult centre for training and research based on the work of Rudolf Steiner. Courses offered include education, environmental design, music, storytelling and

sculpture. Our courses range in length from one day to three years. We run weekend workshops and a summer school annually. Every year we offer an individual retreat from 24 to 31 December (inclusive). Please contact the College for further details.

Bore Place

☑ **Retreats**
☑ **Venue**
☑ **Workshops**
☑ **Bed & Breakfast**
48 bedspaces in 27 rooms

Commonwork
Bore Place
Chiddingstone
Kent
TN8 7AR
Telephone: 01732 463255
Facsimile: 01732 740264
Commonwork, an educational trust, is a centre for conferences, workshops and retreats, on a 500 acre farm in Kentish Low Weald.

Stacklands Retreat House

☑ **Retreats**
20 bedspaces in 20 rooms
Contact: The Administrator
Society of Retreat Conductors
Stacklands Retreat House
West Kingsdown
Sevenoaks
Kent
TN15 6AN
Telephone: 01474 852247

Stacklands, the home of the Society of Retreat Conductors, is an Anglican centre for the study and giving of retreats according to the spiritual exercises of St Ignatius Loyola: a series of scripture-based meditations designed to help the retreatant to become more aware of his or her true self; to become more Christ-centred and to respond more fully to God's love. Send a stamped addressed envelope to the Administrator for a programme.

Aylesford Priory

☑ **Retreats**
☑ **Venue**
☑ **Workshops**
☑ **Bed & Breakfast**
100 bedspaces in 62 rooms
Contact: Margaret Dunk
The Friars
Aylesford Priory
Aylesford
Kent
ME20 7BX
Telephone: 01622 717272
Facsimile: 01622 715575

Home of a community of Carmelite Friars running a programme of retreats. The guesthouse welcomes individuals and groups. Conferences can also be accommodated.

The *Redfield Centre* is an "away-from-it-all" kind of place and yet only 50 miles from London.

Set in the 17 acre estate of the Redfield Community, the residential accommodation is located in a self-contained cottage away from the big house.

Everyone expresses delight at the vegetarian cuisine.

The ideal group size is 16 but we have run certain kinds of events for over 100 people. Give us a ring on *01296 714983* and see if the times that you want are available.

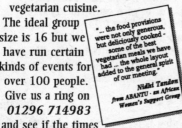

"... the food provisions were not only generous, but deliciously cooked – some of the best vegetarian meals we have had ... the whole layout added to the general spirit of our meeting."

Nidhi Tandon from ABANTU - an African Women's Support Group

REDFIELD

Brakes Coppice Farm

Telham Lane, Battle, East Sussex TN33 0SJ
Tel: 01424 830347

The owners, Michael and Fay Ramsden, specialise in holidays for the elderly.
We will collect our guests door-to-door, take them out in the car during their stay and ensure food is cooked to their liking.
All rooms have en-suite shower, toilet and basin.
Remote control colour tv.
Write or ring for more details

Stacklands Retreat House

Set in over 80 acres of garden and woodland in beautiful Kent countryside, within easy access of London.

Accommodation is in single bed-sitting rooms with hot and cold water. Each floor has its own bathroom and a shower is available.

The main chapel and the dining room are both spacious. There are two smaller chapels; and two sitting rooms, with library. Coffee and tea are available at all times.

Retreats are open to anyone who is searching to know, love and serve God.

Bookings and enquiries to:

The Administrator, Stacklands Retreat House, West Kingsdown, Sevenoaks, Kent TN15 6AN

✆ 01474 852247

Little Grove

Established 1983

A beautiful rural setting one hour from Central London, close to trains and motorways, with good facilities for most types of courses and events.

Non-residential up to 80 people. Simple accommodation for 18 can be extended by camping or other arrangements.

Delicious vegetarian or standard catering provided, or self catering if preferred.

Luxurious warmth in large Sauna. Our rates are low and we are always glad to discuss your needs in detail.
Phone 01494 782720

Greater
London

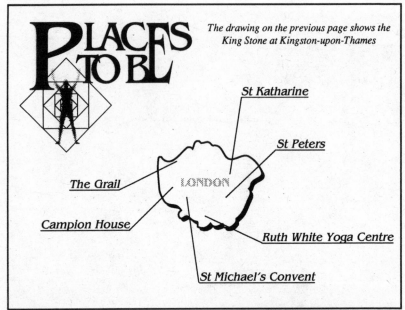

The drawing on the previous page shows the King Stone at Kingston-upon-Thames

St Katharine

St Peters

The Grail

LONDON

Campion House

Ruth White Yoga Centre

St Michael's Convent

Royal Foundation of St Katharine

☑ **Retreats**
☑ **Venue**
☑ **Workshops**
24 bedspaces in 20 rooms
Royal Foundation of St Katharine
2 Butcher Row
London
E14 8DS
Telephone: 0171 790 3540
Facsimile: 0171 702 7603

A gracious eighteenth century house in Stepney offering facilities for retreats and conferences to individuals and groups. Twenty rooms.

Community of St Peters

☑ **Retreats**
☑ **Venue**
6 bedspaces in 4 rooms
Contact: Barbara Deane or Paul Pearson
Community of St Peters
522 (abc) Lordship Lane
East Dulwich
London
SE22 8LD
Telephone: 0181 693 6885

Ecumenical lay community offering quiet days for individuals or groups and a regular cycle of community prayer.

Ruth White Yoga Centre

St Michael's Convent
56 Ham Common
Richmond
Surrey
TW10 7JH
Telephone: 0181 940 8711
Facsimile: 0181 332 2927

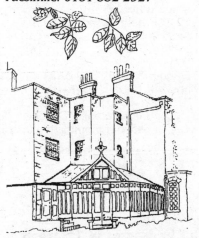

☑ **Retreats**
☑ **Workshops**
☑ **Bed & Breakfast**
40 bedspaces in 30 rooms
Ruth White Yoga Centre
Church Farm House
Springclose Lane
Cheam
Surrey
SM3 8PU
Telephone: 0181 644 0309
Yoga for everyone - offering classes for relaxation, breathing and yoga.

St Michael's Convent

☑ **Retreats**
☑ **Venue**
☑ **Workshops**
17 bedspaces in 15 rooms

With its beautiful four acre garden, the Mother House of the Community of the Sisters of the Church (Anglican) near Richmond Park and the River Thames - provides a haven of peace and quiet, yet is only a short journey from Richmond Station (London Underground and British Rail). We welcome individuals and groups (maximum 30 people) and can accommodate up to 17 people residentially for short periods (some self-catering). We also offer a variety of "programme" events: painting, clowning, music, circle dancing ...

Campion House

☑ **Retreats**
☑ **Venue**
☑ **Workshops**
40 bedspaces in 40 rooms
Campion House
112 Thornbury Road
Osterley
Middlesex
TW7 4NN
Telephone: 0181 568 3821
Facsimile: 0181 569 9645

A House of Prayer based on Ignatian spirituality but open to all Christian denominations.

The Grail

☑ **Retreats**
☑ **Venue**
☑ **Workshops**
32 bedspaces in 17 rooms
Contact: David Coupe
The Grail
125 Waxwell Lane
Pinner
Middlesex
HA5 3ER
Telephone: 0181 866 2195/0505
Facsimile: 0181 866 1408

The Grail Community is one of several branches of the Grail Society which was started in Holland in 1921. This is a Roman Catholic Institute of single and married people, men and women, both young and old. The Society seeks, in an increasingly impersonal world, to promote understanding of the uniqueness and value of each person. The long term community at "Waxwell" consists of women who, choosing to remain single, make a life commitment. The community home is an Elizabethan farmhouse (with library, guest wing and conference extensions) set in ten acres of cultivated and wilderness land. The work of the community includes: support for families and married people; publishing; hospitality; residential courses on arts, religion, human growth, focussing on the spiritual; helping those under stress; and provision of space and solitude for those seeking rest and prayer. Individuals looking for space and quiet can stay in small hermitages in the grounds.

Outside the United Kingdom

The drawing on the previous page shows the menhirs of Lagatjar in north west France

France

Ireland

Lios Dána Holistic Centre

☑ **Retreats**
☑ **Venue**
☑ **Workshops**
☑ **Bed & Breakfast**
18 bedspaces in 8 rooms
Lios Dána Holistic Centre
Inch-Annascaul
County Kerry
Ireland
Telephone: 00 353 66 58189

Beside beach and mountains, offering workshop facilities and individual holidays. Aikido, Shiatsu, Yoga, meditation, Macrobiotic healing available with vegetarian meals.

Le Relais ✓

☑ **Venue**
☑ **Bed & Breakfast**
22 bedspaces in 11 rooms
Contact: Barbara Hubbard
Le Relais
Le Bourg
Pillac
France16390
Telephone: 00 33 45 98 61 04
Facsimile: 00 33 45 98 92 03

Peacefully located in Pillac village with glorious countryside all around. Delightful 12th Century post house converted to provide all modern comforts and amenities whilst retaining all its original charm. Offering eleven bedrooms, five bathrooms plus separate cottage/workroom. Large pool. Lovely covered terrace and mature private gardens. Vegetarian meals.

Le Plessis Vegetarian Guesthouse

☑ **Bed & Breakfast**
8 bedspaces in 3 rooms
Contact: Janine & Steve Judges
Le Plessis
Plumaudan
France 22350
Telephone: 00 33 96 86 00 44

Le Plessis is a vegetarian haven in the beautiful Breton countryside. At one time a working farm, Le Plessis has been recently renovated to combine the charm of the original rustic features of the farmhouse with modern comfort. The atmosphere is relaxed and friendly, a home away from home. We are ideally situated for Channel crossings to St Malo, Caen, Cherbourg and Roscoff. Our nearest town, Dinan, is a magnificent mediaeval fortress town, overlooking an ancient port on the River Rance. We are also within easy reach of many other places of interest, including Merlin's Tomb and the Fountain of Youth in the Forest of Paimpont, Rennes megaliths, as well as the vast sandy beaches of the Côte d'Emeraude. Whether walking, cycling or motoring, our region has much to offer. Excellent vegetarian meals are also on offer. Fresh produce, organic when available, is used to create healthy breakfasts and varied and imaginative three course evening meals, served in generous portions. Whether you stay for two nights or two weeks you will find the food to be of a consistently high standard. We also have a charming self-catering cottage (6 beds in 2 rooms) next door to the guesthouse. Cottage guests are welcome to dine in the guesthouse dining room. Vegans welcome. Reasonable prices. Vegetarian proprietors.

Le Blé en Herbe Rural Retreat

☑ **Retreats**
☑ **Venue**
☑ **Workshops**
☑ **Bed & Breakfast**
8 bedspaces in 3 rooms
Contact: Maria Sperring
Le Blé en Herbe
Puissetier
La Cellette
France 23350
Telephone: 00 33 55 80 62 83

Nestling in the foothills of the Massif Central, Le Blé en Herbe is an Holistic Rural Retreat set in 7.5 acres of gardens, field and woods. Located in La Creuse, Central France - a region known for lakes, green lanes, wild flowers, butterflies and birds of prey - here a peaceful atmosphere flows from living lightly on the Earth. It is a place of enchantment and simplicity, a space to nurture the inner child, shake off the masks of society and commune with the basic Rythms of Nature. The Centre is home to Maria Sperring - gardener, masseuse, student of Yoga - and various friends and helpers. We welcome visitors for B&B, full-board, camping and a range of courses (eg Yoga, dance, Shiatsu, herbalism, massage, voicework). We serve wholefood vegetarian meals with beautiful organic produce fresh daily from the "Sun" garden. Produce is available for sale to self-catering campers. A small green space where time is measured in Circadian Rythms. Le Blé limits course camps to no more than 15 guests. Visits are made by prior arrangement only. Typical rates per day (Summer 1995): B&B 60F; Guest Room with all meals 140F; Camping with all meals 100F; Camping only 15F. Nearest train station is Gueret. 300 miles from Dieppe and Le Havre.

Manoir les Thomas ✓

☑ **Retreats**
☑ **Venue**
☑ **Workshops**
☑ **Bed & Breakfast**
20 bedspaces in 8 rooms
Contact: Helen Caradon
Manoir les Thomas
Grand Castang
Lalinde
France 24150
Telephone: 00 33 53 61 64 69
Facsimile: 00 33 53 24 20 25

Spacious 16th Century Dordogne manor and gardens, meadows, woodland. Offers courses in creative and healing arts, also B&B/full board/camping holidays. Delicious meals, mostly vegetarian. Riding, watersports nearby, prehistoric sites. Gorgeous countryside. Memorable venue, theatre space, craft facilities. Send for full details and current programme.

Domaine de Montfleuri

Contact: Erica Steinhauer
Domaine de Magot
Vabre
France 81330
Telephone: 00 33 63 50 48 02
Facsimile: 00 33 63 50 48 42

☑ **Venue**
☑ **Workshops**
☑ **Bed & Breakfast**
16 bedspaces in 5 rooms
Contact: Dominique Barron
Domaine de Montfleuri
Bouglon
France 47250
Telephone: 00 33 53 20 61 30

Welcome to Montfleuri! Vegetarian B&B in friendly atmosphere. Montfleuri is a beautiful country house with gardens, swimming pool, panoramic views set in creative peaceful surroundings. An ideal venue for workshops touching personal development, crafts, nature etc ...

Domaine de Magot

☑ **Retreats**
☑ **Venue**
☑ **Workshops**
☑ **Bed & Breakfast**
15 bedspaces in 6 rooms

80 acre wooded oasis in Languedoc National Park. Varied accommodation: farmhouse, tipis and camping. River, waterfall, meadows - unspoilt and breathtakingly beautiful. Vegetarian communal meals mainly from our organic garden. Home-baking and deep-earth spring. Working and non-working holidays, retreats and courses. Children welcome. Raku wood-fired kiln and further craft facilities planned. Simplicity, closeness to nature with the chance to learn, to teach, to share within the Garden. Long-term stays available and negotiable. Plans include restoration of buildings - builders etc welcome; much woodland work too! Gypsy caravan to restore; herb garden to establish. A motley crew of kindred spirits all seeking simplicity,

reconnection and beauty.
Wilderness is healing. Also
contactable at 01865 251620
(Telephone) and 01865 251134
(Facsimile).

Spain

Cortijo Romero

☑ **Retreats**
☑ **Venue**
☑ **Workshops**
22 bedspaces in 11 rooms
Cortijo Romero
care of Little Grove
Grove Lane
Chesham, Buckinghamshire
HP5 3QQ
Telephone: 01494 782720
Facsimile: 01494 776066
Small groups with exclusive use
of delightful buildings,
gardens and pool set in an 800
year old olive grove, surrounded
by the magnificent Alpujarras
National Park. Comfortable
rooms, all with bath.

The Sanctuary

☑ **Retreats**
☑ **Venue**
☑ **Workshops**
☑ **Bed & Breakfast**
10 bedspaces in 5 rooms
Contact: Ros Mansell
Cami del Santuari 4
La Plana
Javea   Alicante
Spain 03730
Telephone: 00 34 6646 0732
Holidays offering sun and fun
on a magical headland in
Spain; including yoga, massage,
meditation, art, relaxation, t'ai
chi.

Greece

Skyros Centre - Atsitsa

☑ **Retreats**
☑ **Workshops**
160 bedspaces in 80 rooms
Skyros Centre
care of 92 Prince of Wales Road
London
NW5 3NE
Telephone: 0171 267 4424
Facsimile: 0171 284 3063

Holidays for mind, body and spirit on beautiful Greek island. Yoga, windsurfing, art, personal development, writers' workshops with Sue Townsend etc.

Many locations

Vegiventures

Contact: Nigel Walker
Castle Cottage
Castle Square
Castle Acre
Norfolk
PE32 2AJ
Telephone: 01760 755888

Holidays and houseparties with great vegetarian/vegan food. Venues include: Crete, Peru, the English Lake District and Wales. Phone for a free brochure.

Domaine de Magot

☆ a healing unspoilt corner of Languedoc/Gaia ...
☆ retreats, working holidays, courses etc ... also available for hire for courses, gatherings etc

DOMAINE de MAGOT (DD)	40 Cowley Road
VABRE 81330	Oxford
FRANCE	OX41 1HZ
✆ 00 33 63 50 48 02	✆ 01865 251620

Cortijo Romero

Alternative Holidays in Spain
since 1986

A stunningly beautiful, unspoilt environment - mountains, rivers, sea, ancient villages and the fabled city of Granada

Workshops by some of the finest people in the Human Potential movement worldwide

325 sunshine days annually - open all year

Masses of flowers, palm trees, luscious orchards and shaded courtyards

**Phone for a brochure
01494 782720**

Index by
Name

A

B

C

D

E

F

G

H

I

J

K

L

M

N

O

P

Q

R

S

Communal Living

If you've enjoyed this book then you'll probably enjoy *Diggers and Dreamers - the Guide to Communal Living*. Produced every two years, *D&D* contains an up-to-date Directory of British communal living groups - of all types. There is also an international listing and a Resource section containing references to useful books and organisations.

If you're interested in joining a community, starting one up ... or just visiting ... then the articles in *D&D* will give you a good introduction to the ideas behind communal living and a better insight into how communities do and don't work.

D&D is available in bookshops but it's often easier to get it by mail order. You can order from:
Edge of Time Ltd
PO Box 1808
Winslow
Buckingham
MK18 3RN

should be available until mid 1995. It contains articles on:
- a self-build hamlet in Shropshire
- a permaculture village in Australia
- community building principles
- the movement towards a green society
- historical articles about communalism in the first half of the 20th Century
- Twin Oaks Community in the United States

plus a couple of hilarious glimpses of life in a fictitious Borsetshire commune

Send your order with a cheque for £10 payable to "Edge of Time Ltd".

The Guide to Communal Living

should be available from the late Summer of 1995. Articles pencilled in at the time of writing include:
- punks and communes
- communities and social change
- artists in communities
- how visitors get treated
- design in communities
- cult hysteria
- setting up and financing communities
- communalism in the post war years
- the communal background of Walter Segal - self-build housing pioneer

Mail order price not yet fixed but likely to be £10. Cheques should be payable to "Edge of Time Ltd"

*Dear Reader, We hope that you have found **Places to BE 95/96** to be both useful and enjoyable. We welcome your feedback and invite you to fill out this postcard and return it to us. No stamp is required. In return we'll be offering you a discount on the next edition.*

Please tick one or both

❏ I run/organise workshops/courses ❏ I participate in workshops/courses

What are you looking for most from a directory like this? Please score (1 = first)

☐ individual retreats ☐ group retreats ☐ venues to hire

☐ led workshops ☐ "alternative" B&Bs ☐ working holidays

☐ .... ☐ .... ☐ ....

What features would you add to a future edition?

How did you hear about Places to BE?

Name

Address

Postcode

❏ We will continue to mail you about this and other publications distributed by *Edge of Time* unless you tick this box

*Do you run or do you know of a venue not listed in **Places to BE 95/96**? Make sure that we know about that venue when we come to compile **Places to BE 97/98**.*
Fill out this postcard and return it to us. No stamp is required.

Name of venue

Address

Postcode

Telephone number

Fax number

Contact Name

How did you hear about Places to BE?

2

PO Box 1808
Winslow
Buckinghamshire
MK18 3BR

2

PO Box 1808
Winslow
Buckinghamshire
MK18 3BR